Charla — Hey, I ___

you enjoy these stories

from Duluth's hillside!

D1288459

ABOUT THE AUTHOR

Don Ness grew up during the 1980s and '90s as a shy pastor's kid in the Hillside, a working-class Duluth neighborhood of modest homes and spectacular Lake Superior views. Coming of age amid decades of decline for the city powerfully affected Don, and as a young man he committed himself to public service. After eight years as a city councilor, he was elected Duluth's mayor. Even though he struggled early and made a string of unpopular decisions, Duluth residents eventually gave him job-approval ratings around 89 percent, *Twin Cities Business* named him 2013 Person of the Year, and Garrison Keillor once called him "America's most popular mayor." During his sixteen years in elected office, Don has contributed to and celebrated his hometown's revitalization and truly believes its best days are yet to come. Don and Laura Ness and their three kids—Eleanor, James, and Owen—live happily in a city built on a hill overlooking the world's greatest lake.

Hillsider: Snapshots of a Curious Political Journey

Essays, anecdotes, illustrations, a bit of verse, and a bunch of photographs
reflecting on a young elected official's adventures in Duluth municipal elections,
city governance, live music, craft beer, mountain biking, and more embarrassing
public life and political lessons than a book this size ought to include.

Copyright © 2015 Don Ness. All rights reserved. Except for short excerpts for
review purposes, no part of this book may be reproduced or transmitted in any
form by any means, electronic or mechanical, including photocopying, without
permission in writing from the publisher.

All copyrights belong to their respective owners.

Cover design by Joe Gunderson. Front cover image by outdoor photographer
extraordinaire Hansi Johnson.

Printed in the USA by JS Print Group
10 9 8 7 6 5 4 3 2 1 0 First Edition

ISBN-13: 978-0-692-49012-9
ISBN-10: 0-692-49012-4

Hillside Publishing
P.O. Box 2
Duluth, MN 55801

ANDREA PETERSON, ART DIRECTOR & BOOK DESIGNER

Andrea lives in Hermantown, just outside Duluth. That could have meant the demise of her partnership on this project if Mayor Ness weren't open, every once in a while, to welcoming outsiders from up the hill into his city's world.

After a few years as a teacher, Andrea started building what has become a 15-year graphic-design career. She also authored, illustrated, and designed a six-book phonemic awareness curriculum (which she doesn't mind shamelessly plugging, and which you can learn more about at www.funemics.com).

Andrea and her husband live with their six kids on five acres in the country, but she always cherishes seeing Lake Superior's expansive vistas as she commutes over the hill and into town on her daily trips to the grocery store.

ACKNOWLEDGEMENTS

In December 2014, I came up with the completely unreasonable idea to self-publish this book. It required time and talent that I didn't (and still don't) possess. I wanted it to feature modern design, original art, and photography. I could not personally deliver on any of those elements.

If the book enjoys any success, it'll be due to the amazing talents of and contributions from dozens of friends who all chipped in to make my unreasonable idea a reality.

Very few political books feature the design you'll find here. The most important partner I've had in this project is my friend, art director, and designer Andrea Peterson. She's the hero of this story. Each of these 304 pages required Andrea's skillful touch and sense of style. What you don't see are the hundreds and hundreds of pages of concepts she and I considered then dismissed; the radical changes to her already excellent design ideas; the dozens of times we shuffled the order of these pages to give this mosaic narrative its shape. Andrea has remained strongly committed, forgivingly patient, and relentlessly positive, even when the hours grew long and the details became painstaking. Her incredible insight allows the book's design to lift up its stories.

And then there are the stories themselves. At the start of the project, I assumed I could simply take my vast collection of speeches, editorials, and notebooks full of ideas and plop them into book form. Easy-peasy. I quickly realized how naïve that idea was. Writing is hard. Writing short is even harder. Writing short for publication in a book that my grandchildren will read? Paralyzingly difficult.

Fortunately for me, Chris Godsey and Jessica Tillman became my primary editors. They saved the project. Their sharp eyes for grammatical detail, their imaginative word choices, and their intuitive understanding of what I was struggling to convey felt like magic. Over the past seven months, Andrea, Chris, and Jessica have become my book family, and I cannot adequately express how much they mean to me.

While the immediate book family is relatively small, the extended family is huge. Anna Tennis in particular contributed striking wit and poetic styling to what have become my favorite essays. Paul Lundgren, Lucie Amundsen, Julie Zenner, Patrick Ness, Mary Ness, Cal Benson, Wendy Webb, Eric Gustafson, and Laura Ness all gave a tremendous amount of thoughtful feedback and brilliance, which ultimately shaped the elements into a much stronger, more cohesive compilation.

Other writers, including Garrison Keillor, Louis Jenkins, Maria Bamford, Nate LaCoursiere, Pat Francisco, and Paul Lundgren, also contributed pieces to the book.

Some of my favorite local photographers contributed extraordinary images that tell enigmatic stories beyond words. Photos are the soul of the book. These photographers manage to capture the complex character(s) of Duluth that merit(s) celebration. You'll likely find yourself keeping a thumb on the photo index in the back of the book to find out who captured each image you come upon.

Gifted artists Chris Monroe, Brian Barber, Bridget Riversmith, Beau Walsh, and Joe Klander contributed original art specifically created for the book. You'll also find paintings by Michael Biwarer, Arna Rennan, Alison Aune-Hinkel, and several works by painter Adam Swanson.

We have relied heavily on the expertise of talented professionals such as our printer Tobbi Stager, whose attention to minute detail has elevated this self-published book to the level of a professional publication. Joe Gunderson donated his immense talent to our cover design, and James Monroe brought book-publishing expertise to our team. And thank-you to my brother-in-law Rick Gierczic of Bagaki Enterprises for his excellent web services.

Our successful Kickstarter campaign allowed us to make modest payments to dozens of talented contributors. Please see page 280 for a word on the impact of the campaign and a thank-you to our supporters.

Dozens of other people have provided needed support and understanding throughout this challenging process. For the past seven months, I have dedicated nearly every spare moment I have to this project. I have been up late almost every evening, writing and editing the text. Book details have consumed my weekends. Many thanks to my family, co-workers, and friends, who have graciously withstood my sleep-deprived and stress-induced crankiness.

More than anyone, I want to thank my wife Laura and my kids Ella, James, and Owen for their patient and loving support over these past seven months. They have borne the brunt of this unreasonable undertaking, and now that it's complete I intend to make it up to them.

Many other people deserve my thanks for their part in supporting and inspiring this process. Thank you. 🌉

THANKS TO A GREAT TEAM

Many thanks to (from top left, previous page): Jessica Tillman, Chris Godsey, Anna Tennis, Derek Montgomery, Julie Zenner, Brian Barber, Joe Gunderson, Craig Chilcote, Chris Monroe, Dennis O'Hara, Paul Lundgren, Michael K. Anderson; (this page) Joe Klander, Brian Rauvola, Kip Praslowicz, Andy Miller, Lucie Amundsen, Tobbi Stager, Hansi Johnson, Jess Belwood, and Rich Narum; (not pictured) Alison Aune-Hinkel, Maria Bamford, Cal Benson, Michael Biwarer, Pat Francisco, Rick Gierczic, Eric Gustafson, Louis Jenkins, Garrison Keillor, Nathan LaCoursiere, James Monroe, Laura Ness, Mary Ness, Patrick Ness, Arna Rennan, Bridget Riversmith, Adam Swanson, Beau Walsh, and Wendy Webb.

Photography contributors: Clint Austin, Adam Bettcher, John Biasi, Taylor Bjork, Jeremiah Brown, Deb Carrol, Tim Clay, Sam Cook, Don Davis, Walt Dizzo, Dan Dresser, Larry Dunlap, Jon Dyess, Steve Forslund, Preflash Gordon, Brett Groehler, Jake Gunderson, John Hatcher, John Heino, Zach Kerola, Kenneth Kollodge, Bob King, Sarah Krueger, Steve Kuchera, Scott Lunt, Maxwell McGruder, Nate Minor, Becca Moen, Aaron Molina, Luke Nadeau, Jeff Peabody, Hattie Peterson, Kim Randolph, Rene Rhodman, John Schadl, Amanda Teague, Shawn Thompson, John Trueman, Ivy Vainio, Anne Victoria, Brandon Wagner, Paul Walsh, Barry Yanowitz, Naomi Yaeger-Bischoff.

For

Laura Ness

Eleanor Ness

James Ness

Owen Ness

Don Ness, Sr.

Mary Ness

and the 86,000+ residents of Duluth,
the vast majority of whom are not named Ness.

HILLSIDER

[SNAPSHOTS OF A CURIOUS
POLITICAL JOURNEY]

Essays, anecdotes, illustrations, a bit of verse, and a bunch of photographs
reflecting on a young elected official's adventures in Duluth municipal elections,
city governance, live music, craft beer, mountain biking, and more embarrassing
public life and political lessons than a book this size ought to include.

——————— BY ———————

DON NESS

FOREWORD

by Laura Ness

I love an unusual man. I've always wanted to write that one-liner. But it's true, really. Donny is unusual. He's a lot of things that shouldn't usually go together easily or well.

When I first met Donny he was a lanky long strider, always distracted, and slow to smile. It's hard to say what drew me in closest, but a particular mental snapshot stands out. I caught a glimpse of him walking down the street. A swift clip, his dark and dramatic eyebrow half-cocked. It was likely the expression on his face—that inscrutable look of deep reflection—that was so curious to me. It attracted me then and has kept me hooked all these years.

Donny is an old-fashioned man with many seemingly contradictory characteristics. He is soft spoken, but his words are often the weightiest in a room. He is nonjudgmental and unassuming—my two possibly favorite things about him—but he maintains very high standards of conduct for himself. He is rock-solid steady, but when a good plan emerges he will advocate for change without delay. He's a passionately committed mayor and a terrifically devoted dad.

I think we both have been somewhat surprised by Donny's local celebrity status. Sometimes people ask me—occasionally with a piercing gaze, other times in a more offhand way—what it's like being married to the mayor. I usually struggle to find a response, because just like everyone else, our life is what it is, and we do our best with what we've been given. (We did meet a king and queen, once. That was pretty cool.)

The truth is that some things have been hard. I struggled for a long time to be myself and make peace with my shortcomings. The position reveals myriad opportunities to agonize over missteps and faux pas, and I'll never feel we've done enough with the gifts we've been given.

We have, as often as possible, tried to honor opportunities to live in this community in the most essential, human ways: getting invited to picnics and dinners and fundraisers and parties, or being stopped in the Whole Foods Co-op by people who just want to know how we're doing. It's all been the most humbling and amazing way to be a part of so many wonderful and interesting lives. I know

I'm only scratching the surface of this phenomenon, as both Donny and I are fairly introverted, and we could never have reciprocated or expressed the full extent of our appreciation.

It's been the great gift of my life to share some part of Donny's unusual story. He downplays his success, attributing much of it to serendipitous timing and a receptive audience. I likely reinforce that notion because, even though I love and admire Donny, I too am most interested in celebrating this chapter of Duluth's progress as a story of organic collaboration, contributions, and successes. Duluth was ready for a galvanizer, a doer, a thinker. We are so fortunate that Donny is who he is. And we are equally fortunate that people of this region are who they are: hard workers, dedicated stewards, critical thinkers, and each, in his or her own way, dreamers.

I felt terribly nervous when Donny asked me to write this foreword. I am a sensitive and quiet sort. I expected him to ask someone whose words would convey an illuminating artistry or insight that would put his life and career into impeccable context. But he asked me to write it, and I know and love that he accepts, understands, and genuinely appreciates who I actually am. He is perfectly okay with my unassuming and unambitious ways, so I've just tried to share a bit of my perspective. While writing, I've become aware that my view of this everyday we share, with its unique complexities and challenges, is art enough.

I hope you enjoy this book for what it is: a collection of stories from a modern hometown boy. More often than not these days, we leave the towns we grew up in. Donny's commitment to Duluth is unusual—it coaxed from him a great gift of leadership, and called him to serve in positions he might otherwise have never aspired to. That deep commitment has served Duluth well.

I appreciate the book's eclectic nature. It lends itself to a straight-through read, dog-earing with abandon, or a leisurely flip-through. I really enjoy Donny's essays, especially the ones that discuss his political and leadership styles, but I have to admit my favorite pages are those that feature our little ones, who are dang cute and interesting. Yes, Ella, you're just too lovely; James, you're a wild and wonderful young man; and Owen, you are such a sweetheart.

Duluth, we love you. We thank you for the incredible years you've given us in the mayor's office.

INTRODUCTION

Hey! Welcome to my book! I'm so glad you stopped by. Please, please, come right on in.

Can I offer you anything? A political essay? An original illustration? Maybe an embarrassing personal story or two? Water? Mi libro es tu libro.

Oh man, I hope you like what we've done. Before I show you around, keep in mind that I am a politician … writing a book about myself. You see what I'm saying, right? You should definitely lower your expectations. Lower …. Lower …. Even lower than that. There you go. Just north of contempt. Perfect.

So, let me show you around.

You're probably used to seeing books with "structure" and "cohesive organization." One interesting thing about this book is that it has very little of either. Instead, we basically gathered a big pile of stuff—a bunch of personal anecdotes and observations, political-philosophy screeds, original art and illustrations, and some other words and images that defy description—sorted them according to three, five-year periods of my life, and called it good.

Section I of the book follows a young, idealistic politico embarking on a strange new adventure. Section II tells tales of his darkest days, when all hope seems lost. Section III shows a community rallying to define a better future. It's essentially the original *Star Wars* trilogy, only in the much more bizarre galaxy of home-rule-charter municipal government.

It might look like a colorful mess at first, and I guess it kind of is, but here's a convenient justification: the randomness reflects my experience as mayor. During an average day, I might start by leading a serious policy meeting, jump to reading to preschoolers, take a call to help someone through a tough personal matter, and then head straight to a ribbon-cutting ceremony celebrating a new development and job growth. Life as mayor moves among personal, professional, and community roles so quickly that it can be tough (and probably not useful) to discern the difference.

Too many pieces are missing for this to be an autobiography or even a memoir. Too many hugely important events are just not mentioned. Even the serious issues that come up aren't given the time and attention they truly deserve. This book is a relatively small collection of visual and textual snapshots—enough to show a bit about some interesting things that happened, but not nearly enough to tell the full story.

I especially wish we had more space for celebrating people. I wanted to highlight hundreds of my favorite friends and community leaders with glowing profiles and gorgeous photos. For about a month I struggled mightily to do it—to write short, interesting pieces about all the people I love and admire. But every time I felt like the list was complete, I'd feel like I was leaving someone out. And while I'm comfortable telling tales on myself, some stories that involve other folks just aren't mine to tell. I knew what I wanted to do, but I couldn't see how to do it as well as it deserves to be done. So I reluctantly but wisely scaled back. I wish I wouldn't have had to.

Aaanywho, get a load of those gorgeous photos! Aren't they spectacular? And I know you'll also love the original art up ahead by some of my favorite local painters and illustrators. You'll come across a lot of local music in here, too.

Oh, careful. Those are incredibly brittle. I like to call them my "humors," but they're so dry most normal people just see them as odd constructs. They certainly don't hold up well to close examination. Even a lingering gaze can cause them to completely disintegrate. Best to take them in quickly, not think about them too deeply, and move right along.

Ha! Did you just say, "That's different…"? Funny you should use that phrase, because that used to be the title of this book! And you said it with such scorn and passive aggressiveness—that's exactly what we were going for. This paragraph was much funnier with the previous title. In spite of changing the title to *Hillsider* I've kept this joke because I can't afford to lose even one sorta, kinda funny idea.

There's probably some really good reason why other political books aren't set up this way. Luckily I didn't know any better, so here we are! 🌉

Don Ness
Duluth, MN
6/20/2015

Section I

In which a boyishly earnest and naïve young man learns
painful, embarrassing, and public political lessons
while seeking adventure in city governance.

Ages 25-30 | 2000-2005

DULUTH

This city is brutally indifferent and seductively welcoming.

It builds loyalty and demands struggle.

It pushes you away as intensely as it pulls you in.

"HILLSIDER"

Well we ain't got, much money

Ain't got fancy cars

But we got some bouncing babies

Bouncing 'round in the yard

And you might know, someplace better

For all I know it's true

But I got ten bucks in my pocket, boys

And a million dollar view

Lyrics by Jamie Ness, performed by the Boomchucks

DEFINING MEMORY

It was a short jaunt home from my second grade classroom. I needed to change out of my school clothes and hustle over to Central Field for a pickup game of baseball. I bounded up the wooden stairs, my Spider-Man lunch box in hand. I burst into a scene that would leave a permanent impression.

I flew through the door and was caught in mid-flight. A massive mountain of a man was folded onto himself, crying in grief and anxiety. My parents had placed their hands on his shoulders, praying for him and his family. He had been laid off and had no idea how he was going to support his family.

It wasn't unusual to find my parents counseling members of our church family in our living room. As kids, we were well trained to recognize a sensitive situation and either head back outside or hustle up to our bedrooms. But this time I couldn't look away.

It was my first exposure to the complex pain of adult life. The first time I understood how an abstract concept like the economy could leave a pillar of our church community broken in my mom and dad's living room. A formative lesson about both the devastating impact of that recession and the importance of my parents' roles in supporting people through tragedies.

My parents had dedicated their lives to helping others: the church, the battered women's shelter, the children's home, and kids who had been abused or neglected. They had made a lifelong commitment to help people in desperate situations and show them God's grace through patience, kindness, insight, and love.

Can you find the 12 grunge-era clichés?

1. Greasy, wavy hair—"The Chandler"
2. Pimple resulting from proximity to greasy hair
3. KICK!—a Mountain Dew ripoff that was supposedly "extreme"
4. Backwoods mini cigars (fruit flavored)
5. Extra pale skin via extended darkened-room brooding
6. Garage-sale flannel—appropriately unwashed
7. Gold (color) chain
8. X-Large baggy T-shirt featuring a distressed man and the words "Hyper Zone"
9. Underdeveloped soul patch
10. *Catcher in the Rye* (of course) tucked under left arm
11. Detached, anti-establishment look of resentment and defiance toward a world that didn't understand our generation, etc.
12. Diet Rite!!!!

"She said I was afraid of success, which may in fact be true, because I have a feeling that fulfilling my potential would really cut into my sittin' around time."

—Comedian and Duluth native Maria Bamford

A gritty, bone-deep rhythm pumps like a brooding heart, the only semblance of order in the chaotic scene. The singer—a skinny, white Mormon boy holding a battered electric guitar and apparently experiencing some sort of controlled fit—screams into an antique harmonica microphone that scratches and distorts his voice. His face is purple. His eyes, nearly rolled back in their sockets, suggest he is seeing things you don't. His band mates—one on drums, one on rhythm guitar—watch him closely while generating a deep, ominous gravelly groove no two humans seem capable of creating or sustaining.

The long, narrow bar has become a living thing, writhing and twisting, expanding and contracting—the room thrums. Its legal capacity has easily been doubled. Blue cigarette-smoke haze couples with human-sweat humidity to create a mysterious, noxious atmosphere. Personal space doesn't exist near the stage. For at least fifteen layers back, bodies press randomly and sway in involuntary swells. Buck-apiece Black Label beer cans get stomped and kicked and crushed on a black-and-white tile floor slick with mud and booze and sweat.

Sparhawk knows what he's doing, and you trust him.

You know what he's doing to you and you wait for it while just wanting it to happen over and over again. The anticipation is euphoric, visceral, and miserable. You make eye contact with a friend across the room and give a stoic nod to acknowledge the moment, the anticipation, and the chaos to come.

Tension, already more tight and thick than you think you can stand, keeps building. He's got us where he wants us. It's time.

In response to a signal none of the rest of us see, his mates keep driving the beat but back off the volume just slightly. His guitar goes silent.

"My naaaaaaaaaaaaaaame," he wails over their work, drawing out the declaration till you're sure he'll drop from lack of oxygen, "Is ChickenboneGeorge!"

The declaration is punctuated with a chainsaw crash of punk blues. The room explodes in a tangle of limbs jumping, spinning, pushing, pulling. The swells turn to waves crashing angrily into the unforgiving brick walls and against the three-foot-tall stage.

Sparhawk throws his entire body into the obscure lyrics like a rural preacher possessed with the spirit, "They saaaaaaaaaaaaayyyyy … I'm ablackeyedsnake!"

The crowd may combust. And now the mic is out of its stand and Sparhawk is swinging it in great, violent circles and it smashes into the filthy suspended ceiling, unleashing a toxic cloud of tile, dust, and rat shit onto the frothy crowd.

They play that way for at least another hour and during that time, in that room, it's like we were always this way. It's like we've arrived here together for a reason, to have exactly this experience.

TWENTYSOMETHING CRISIS

I was a boomerang kid before it was a thing. I "celebrated" my twenty-fifth birthday at my mom and dad's house, sitting on my childhood bed. My parents had graciously welcomed me back into their home so I could live my self-imposed poverty more comfortably. They loved and encouraged me. They never made me feel bad about being there.

But all I could do was feel bad for myself.

My friends were leaving town to start careers and graduate school. I was happy for them, but I also felt abandoned. My understanding of how life works was evaporating. I had no clue how to start adult life.

I mean, how do you do *that*? 🚗

FOG NARROWS OUR HORIZON

For decades, Duluth felt stuck in an impenetrable fog of stagnation and zero-sum turf battles. Negative energy organized into a stifling cloud of pessimism that limited the scope of our imagination.

Even the most positive and pro-Duluth voices felt a need to qualify their optimistic thoughts. We so desperately wanted to be proud of Duluth, but without a positive outlet, that pride often morphed into ugly cynicism.

Leaders of the '80s and '90s saved Duluth from economic devastation that consumed other small Rust Belt cities of that era. It was a remarkable accomplishment.

But staving off crisis isn't the same as fulfilling a greater sense of purpose. The effort exhausted us emotionally and wound up infecting our collective psyche with negativity.

INSPIRATION

Six months after turning twenty-five, I finally moved into my own apartment. Just like that, the world was alive with opportunity. My mind raced in exploration. I'd sit on my dusty corduroy couch and fill notebook after notebook with quotes and ideas that shaped my emerging philosophy and stoked my imagination.

Thumbing through those tattered pages, I am touched by the melodramatic earnestness of it all:

> *Duluth is at a crossroads. One path is a comfortable stroll that leads to our demise. The other embraces a dynamic character, faces challenges head on, and is purposefully aggressive toward the future.*

> *We need leadership uncorrupted by cynicism—instead motivated by idealism.*

> *We need to adapt to a changing world and respond honestly instead of with nostalgia. Nostalgia is a self-inflicted wound in the effort to lead in a rapidly changing world.*

Melodramatic or not, these zealous scratches stirred an inspiration to test my ideas on the most significant stage available. I decided to run for city council.

CAMPAIGN ANNOUNCEMENT

"If you're supporting me, you have great courage and no political instincts whatsoever."

—former Massachusetts Senator Paul Tsongas

I was fond of using this quote during those early campaign events. It was funny because it was true. My brother Patrick recalls the campaign's first moments:

"I came home from St. Cloud to attend the press conference launching Donny's first city council campaign. While he nervously thought about his comments, we lugged a massive wooden lectern up the city hall steps, where the announcement was to take place. We were doing our best to be gentle with the heavy-yet-fragile monstrosity, but the moment we set it down, the entire thing collapsed, clattering loudly against the granite steps.

"Donny stood there smiling and sweating, clearly embarrassed, in the midday sun. Had the scene not seemed so ominous, it would've been a hilarious preface to a political career that hadn't even officially started.

"We felt thankful for another failure that prevented the lectern incident from being more embarrassing than it could have been—the conference failed to attract even a single reporter, so no cameras were there to document the crash. Donny stumbled through his notes for the eight friends and family who had gathered. We all assured him things would improve as the campaign went on. It would have been difficult for them to get worse."

"There are risks and costs to action.
But they are far less than the long-range risks of comfortable inaction."

—John F. Kennedy

We needed a brochure photo of candidate Ness confidently talking with a constituent. There was just one problem: I was terrified to ask anyone to pose. (I mean, what if they said no? I didn't think I could handle the rejection.) Finally, I conjured up the courage to ask this kind Duluthian. Fortunately, Grandma Marge agreed.

SEEKING CONVERSATION

The ideas banging around in my mind were underdeveloped and poorly articulated. The well-traveled path of preformed and memorized talking points felt safe but stifling. So I decided to put my enthusiasm and newfound idealistic passion at center stage in my campaign. Would voters forgive my stumbles if they sensed my sincerity? I was willing to take that risk.

Consultants advise candidates to give convenient answers to complicated questions. I wanted to ask inconvenient questions with complicated answers. Answers I didn't have. I just wanted to start conversations.

I figured if I had any chance of expressing my strengths, I couldn't be afraid of exposing my weaknesses. They were too closely bound. Everyone expected me to lose this race, and that was liberating. I felt free to run the campaign without the pressure of conforming to others' expectations.

Thus began my career-long love affair with low expectations.

NERD NIGHT

Every politician enjoys the support of a core constituency—those voters whose personal or ideological backgrounds most strongly align with their own. These groups become our security blankets of support. They're the folks who will understand when the rest of the world turns against us.

One politician's core constituency might be corporate-business types. Another's might be labor leaders and union members. Others might have core constituencies made up of environmentalists, Tea Party activists, hunters and anglers, or arts advocates. In every example, the politician's core constituency shows something about the politician.

My core constituency? Nerds.

Forget the nerd or geek stereotypes from '80s teen comedies. That's not what I'm talking about. My people, modern nerds, are defined by their sincere enjoyment of serious, complicated and intellectually stimulating content.

Every constituency believes their ideology could solve the world's problems if everyone else would just agree with them. So I acknowledge my personal bias when I proclaim that there is a *very* strong argument for turning the nation's leadership over to the nerds.

Imagine this! What if the membership of Congress were dominated by nerds rather than millionaires? What if Americans started voting for candidates based on nerdy qualities (like understanding policy and nurturing a deep love for spreadsheets) rather than how they look on TV? What if we redirected the analytical power of nerds from Minecraft to statecraft? Imagine the possibilities!

The nerds among us must rise up and saturate government with nerdery. I hereby call for a Nerd Revolution in American politics. Power to the nerds!

SECRET NERD MESSAGE

Hello, normal people. You must find this page of random symbols quite strange. A very odd choice by the author to include it, don't you agree? If so, you should probably just go on to the next essay.

(Psst, hey nerds. Now that we've gotten rid of the others, we can talk about our nerd plans for taking over the world. The following encoded message contains special instructions. If you don't understand it, please see the previous paragraph.)

Donny in high school.
Not a costume.

IMPENDING DOOM

Journal 11-6-99: *After the initial shock of learning that I had won the race, I felt an overwhelming, almost debilitating sense of impending doom.*

During the five months of my city council campaign, I had joyfully promoted my idealism and fresh perspective. But I had yet to convince myself I could actually do the job. I believed strongly in the importance of my ideas. I just wasn't sure I could translate those ideas into quality public service.

The vulnerability that served me well during the campaign now became an easy target for opponents. My notorious sensitivity became a liability in Duluth's bare-knuckle politics. My plan to ignore those tactics was already proving futile.

I had run a blue-sky campaign, but now I felt a storm front gathering energy.

"This," I thought to myself, "could go badly."

SAM SOLON

Sam Solon, my most valued and important political mentor, was dying. He had been battling cancer for more than a year, and now the disease was taking control. For many years, Sam and I had talked almost every day he was in Duluth. I loved our conversations. I peppered him with questions about issues at the legislature, Duluth history, and community power dynamics. He was always patient and generous with his time and his detailed answers.

As a state senator, Sam was known to be smart, tough, and pragmatic. His priority was always whatever was best for Duluth. He loved this city. The most important lesson I learned from Sam was that in local politics, community should always trump ideology.

I had arranged for a professional video team to record a conversation between Sam and me. I planned to give his family a copy and keep one to remember my friend and mentor. We spoke for more than two hours on a wide variety of subjects. He conjured memories of his modest upbringing in the Observation Hill neighborhood—as part of a Greek family in "Little Italy." He recalled his first steps into politics, the excitement of helping pass the Minnesota Miracle, and the projects for which he proudly fought.

Sam let his guard down during taping. He spoke from the heart with the urgency of a man whose time was running short. It was a beautiful and heartbreaking experience.

Days later, the video company called to apologetically explain they had lost all of the audio. I was devastated. I tried desperately to schedule another taping, but Sam and I both knew the moment could not be recreated.

He grew weaker. Two months later, Duluth lost its greatest champion.

"Tell me and I forget, teach me and I may remember, involve me and I learn." —Benjamin Franklin

THE DOTYS

The top left picture was taken just moments after I was first sworn in (and a little while before being sworn *at*) as a city councilor. Mayor Gary Doty was beginning his third and final term.

Mayor Doty and I had our political differences, but he was the leader Duluth needed in the 1990s. After decades of turmoil, the city needed to find a deeper and more substantial foundation. Gary exuded stability as mayor: in his politics, his persistence, his faith, and his family.

As the festivities wound down on my first night as councilor and I was about to head back to my empty apartment, Gary and Marcia invited me along to a family gathering. I vividly remember the laughter and love as their immediate and extended family filled a back corner of the Perkins Restaurant on London Road.

When I was elected mayor, Gary and Marcia became important mentors, helping Laura and me find balance between the pressures of public life and the priority we place on family. They understood the unique challenges of striking that balance and were willing to share reflections on their experience with honesty and empathy.

I often reflect on that joyful moment when I came to understand that strong family life and successful political life could be one and the same.

UNEARNED ADVANTAGES

Let's face it, politicians' successes are far too often based on relatively superficial impressions and subconscious biases. As much as I dislike admitting it, I know my physical characteristics (male, white, tall) have been significant factors in getting chances to prove myself.

That same dynamic has been present throughout my life. There have been hundreds, if not thousands, of moments in which I was given the benefit of the doubt or trusted without qualification—times I was given subtle advantage or positive reinforcement during uncertain moments.

There is a painful realization that the very biases that work in my favor are the same ones that limit some people. Every kid deserves the support and reinforcement that I benefited from in life. We should recognize that these biases, which distribute opportunity and encouragement unevenly, are powerful and inherently unfair.

Fortunately, support and encouragement are unlimited, renewable resources that can be delivered as simply as a smile or as seriously as mentorship. Imagine if we gave these gifts freely to every child in this country.

B&B CONTROVERSY

I had a plan! At my very first city council meeting, I'd quietly listen and do as little as councilorly possible. I'd gently ease into my new role without drawing attention to myself. I might have been naïve, but I knew enough to avoid embarrassment and controversy for as long as possible. It was the perfect plan. Fail-safe.

It worked perfectly. For a whole hour. Then it imploded in spectacular fashion.

I'll explain. We were considering a proposal to turn a beautiful historic house at the end of a dead-end street into a bed and breakfast. The folks who owned this charming home wanted it to be a great destination for visitors. Sounds great, right? That's what I thought until a lurking controversy took me by surprise.

Opponents of the B&B were a group of people I knew and cared about: my college professors, my campaign supporters, and well-respected business leaders. They felt the proposal jeopardized the quality and safety of their neighborhood. Dilemma! Should I vote for a project I believed in or vote to satisfy a group of influential leaders?

Unfortunately, I followed my political instincts rather than my commitment to progress. I voted against the proposal and it failed 4-5. I immediately realized it was the wrong decision. I had failed on my very first opportunity to practice integrity in my decision making. The shame was inescapable and kept me awake well into the night.

Many eyes rolled at my second council meeting when I made a motion to reconsider my vote and forced the entire council to vote again. I once again cast the deciding vote, only this time it was in favor of establishing the neighborhood-ruining B&B.

You never forget your first subpoena. The very people I had aimed to placate with my original vote were now so angry they retained a young, aggressive attorney and filed a lawsuit against me, personally. A brusque, large-foreheaded guy shoved the court order at me: "You've been served."

Now, I'm a rule follower, so the city attorney's insistence that I *not* respond to the subpoena filled me with anxiety. Sure enough, taking that advice led to a contempt of court charge. The local media *loved* the young-councilor-already-in-trouble narrative.

A.G. Thomson House Bed & Breakfast

Hey, kid, welcome to elected life. I had managed to make a painful, frustrating exhibit out of my first month in office. Was this all I had to offer? I learned quickly that bumbling isn't quite as charming in office as it can be while campaigning. Real-life consequences hung in the balance. I had to get my act together.

In the end, everything worked out for the best. The charge was eventually dismissed. The A.G. Thomson House has been named Travelers' Choice by Trip Advisor and best B&B in the region by *Midwest Living* magazine.

And that young, aggressive attorney who brought suit against me on behalf of his clients? Eight years later, Gunnar Johnson became my city attorney.

John Hatcher

John Hatcher's surf board

The joy of spectacular failure.

Kenny Kalligher and Jon Donahue during *The Average Guys* 500th episode celebration

AVERAGE GUYS

Most Friday nights in my twenties went like this: I'd pop a delicious Jack's frozen pizza into the oven, crack open a beer, and flip through an issue of *Rolling Stone*. Then, right at 7 o'clock, I'd click on channel 7, Duluth Public Access TV, to watch *The Average Guys*!

The Average Guys was a simple concept. Jonny D and Kenny K spent an hour every week paging through the current sports news and giving their thoughts and moderately informed opinions on everything from high school basketball to the Super Bowl. They finished every one of their 576 shows over the course of 15 years with the brilliant tagline, "It's cool to be average."

In later years, Jon became a friend of mine. I admired how he carried his irrepressible enthusiasm. He was relentlessly and genuinely passionate about everyday life. While battling cancer in his final years, Jon's wholeheartedness never waned.

In a Facebook post, Jon wrote:

> *"You can put the cancer in the man, but you cannot take the fire out of his Soul!!*
> *GOD has BIG plans for me!!"*

BRIDGE SYNDICATE

The Bridge Syndicate—a small group of young professionals dedicated to increasing local civic, cultural, and economic opportunities—struck a nerve in the early 2000s. As its membership grew from ten to five hundred in just one year, young leaders emerged and began to take ownership of Duluth's future. The group's policy objectives led to serious discussions about demographic projections and economic development strategies. Its social objectives led to rock-paper-scissors tournaments and monthly happy hours. The group inspired a generation of leaders to invest their time and talent in civic improvement.

NESS MESS

In 2000, Duluth was on the front line of a nationwide movement to ban smoking in public places. On a personal level, I strongly supported the ban. Live music venues were my second home those days, and I was tired of smelling like an ashtray. But this was a massive policy decision, and I worried about the impact on local businesses.

As soon as the issue was introduced, my fellow councilors rushed to choose sides. The deciding vote was tossed in my lap. I unwisely used my newfound swing-vote popularity to delve into complexities. Attempting to craft a compromise, I explored tweaking legal definitions of bars and restaurants. I sought to split hairs on where people could eat. I eyed up newfangled technologies such as air curtains. All my efforts were sincere and entirely unhelpful.

It turns out not every issue has a reasonable middle ground. When I offered a series of complex amendments, several people in the council chambers held up signs reading, "No Ness Mess!" They were absolutely right. My blind allegiance to compromise resulted in the worst possible option.

After I realized my approach was making things worse, I chose a side and became the most consistent vote in favor of the ban. My compromise-at-all-costs ideology was proving simplistic and clumsy. My learning curve remained at a treacherous pitch.

A TALE OF TWO ASSESSMENTS

We've lost the art of impartially judging political performance. We all start from our individual biases and ideologies. We give politicians on our side the benefit of the doubt, cheer their successes, and dismiss their failures. We judge politicians on the other side harshly, even when their performances actually deserve praise, and we revel in hate and contempt when things go poorly for them.

Those extreme positive and negative judgements can make it tough for politicians to maintain perspective. Hearing supporters gush is always nice. Hearing opponents raise angry voices can feel like an avalanche of negativity.

How supporters react

It's only mostly bad.

I defend you all the time.

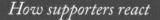

PRETTY BAD   *Actual Political Performance*

(so angry they can hardly speak)

Impeach!

How opponents react

Giving extreme voices attention also gives them power. The tragedy of this dynamic is that elected officials, out of ego and self-preservation, end up spending the vast majority of their energy catering to supporters and marginalizing opponents. 🛎

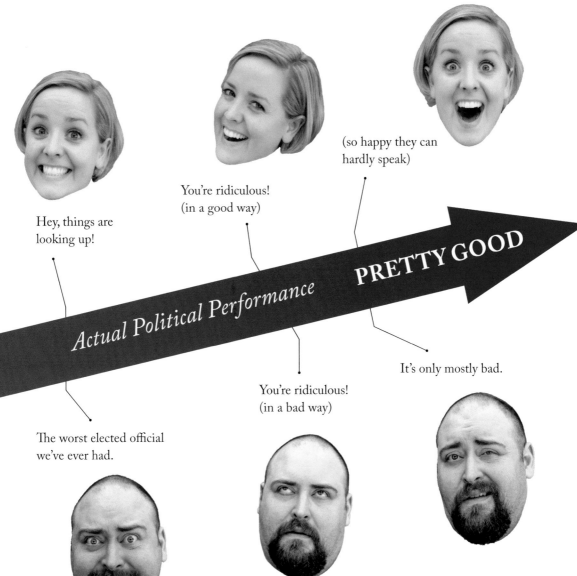

(so happy they can hardly speak)

You're ridiculous! (in a good way)

Hey, things are looking up!

Actual Political Performance PRETTY GOOD

It's only mostly bad.

You're ridiculous! (in a bad way)

The worst elected official we've ever had.

PATRICK DROWNING

"Oh my God. He's going to drown."

A powerful Lake Superior undertow had grabbed my ten-year-old brother, Patrick. He didn't stand a chance as the force pulled him farther from shore. He couldn't touch bottom. His face barely rose above the rough surf as he yelled for help.

My junior-high friend Jeff Isle and I had brought Patrick along with us to Park Point. It was early fall, and a strong easterly wind was pushing massive waves of warm surface water directly into the beach. We jumped and crashed into the waves for hours. But along with the entertaining whitecaps come dangerous riptides like the one that caught Patrick.

He was drowning, and I was to blame. Adrenaline pumped through our veins as we fought the pounding waves to get to him.

When we finally reached him, our relief was short-lived because now all three of us were in danger. The Lake tossed us around. Our lanky limbs flailed in panic as Jeff and I tried to swim Patrick, exhausted and heavy in our arms, toward safety.

Moving parallel to shore, we escaped the undertow and made painfully slow progress toward the beach. Finally we collapsed onto the sand, scared, exhausted, and embarrassed by how close we had come to a devastating tragedy. Truly it was only God's grace that spared Patrick from death and saved me from unbearable grief and remorse.

All my life I have loved The Lake. On that day, I learned to respect it. 🪑

MANY MOODS

Bright, brilliant blue. Sick, miserable grey. Glistening in the sun. Angry waves pounding the rocky shore. Playful sway on a sunny day. Somber stillness under a lingering haze. Beacon of relief on a sweltering August afternoon. Powerful hostility on a brutal November evening. 🛋

JIM OBERSTAR

Congressman Jim Oberstar had just hired me as his campaign manager. It was the Fourth of July, and I was on the Iron Range preparing for five parades and a picnic in six different communities in one day. Obviously, I was terrified. I combed through every detail on the schedule to ensure things would go exactly as planned. I needed to make a good first impression.

I failed before waking up. I had set my alarm for p.m. instead of a.m. and woke up already an hour behind schedule before I could wipe the sleep from my eyes. I recovered a few minutes by driving maniacally to the congressman's house, then surrendered those precious minutes and more when a state patrol officer pulled me over for speeding on our way from Chisholm to Eveleth for the first parade.

For the next six hours, my mistakes caused only annoying inconveniences: a parade spot behind the horses in Eveleth, angry activists complaining about me in Keewatin, and losing Jim for a half hour in Nashwauk.

However, my enjoyment of only moderately bad luck was about to end. While loading our signs into the car on our way to Biwabik for our final parade, I did the unthinkable—I locked the keys in the trunk. It took the AAA guy nearly an hour to get the keys out while my new boss, the United States congressman, stood there in the baking sun. I was crushed. I had failed him. My fledgling professional career was surely done for.

When we finally arrived back at Jim's house late that night, I began a heartfelt apology. He put his hand on my shoulder and wouldn't let me continue. He said, "Donny, this was a very tough day, and you had a lot of things go against you. But you never lost your head." I appreciated this generous and inaccurate assessment.

Then he gave me one of his famous Jim Oberstar bear hugs and said, "Don't worry about this. I'm proud of you." As I began to drive away, I noticed that he was still standing on his front step. He gave me a huge smile and an overhead wave as he shouted, "Happy Independence Day!"

This one moment of grace made me loyal to Jim for a lifetime.

A MAGNIFICENT MIND

Jim Oberstar was one of the brightest minds of our day. His intellect was exceeded only by his unflagging energy and deep, abiding character. Jim was a warm and caring man. He was a good talker, a better listener, and ever ready with a brief anecdote or an off-the-cuff forty-minute speech. His booming voice was always firm, always positive. The longest-serving member of Congress in Minnesota's history, Jim Oberstar served our country with distinction and honor.

"Lumbersexual: Young and middle-aged male urbanites whose sartorial choices are characterized by thick and well-groomed beards, styled haircuts, and clothing that tends towards the rugged. There is a pronounced emphasis on practice of physical craft, obscure skill-sets, and old-timey traditions and methods of manufacture."

—Urbandictionary.com

LUMBERSEXUALS

Let's get real. They're basically cheap rip-offs of a "trend" started by men who worked mines, forests, docks, and ships in and around Duluth a long time ago. Those long-ago guys just wore and did what their jobs and lives required. A few decades later, bored dudes in Portland and Brooklyn thought it would be neat to adopt an "authentic" style that looks cool while riding fixed-gear bicycles and listening to vinyl records by bands you've probably never heard of.

Fortunately for America, Duluth still serves as the country's vanguard, and our geography and economy provide fertile ground for many trendy lumbersexual-related identities including entre-lumber-neurs, craft beer lum-brewers, and lumb-ar-tists. Sadly, some young or middle-aged Duluth men are unem-lumber-ployed. We've also got some lumberjacks, which we often refer to as "loggers." You can observe all these and other trends in their pure Duluth form now, before they reach the coastal cultural wastelands we've dismissively labeled "fly-to country."

Honestly, you'll probably be able to observe them a few decades from now, too, because here's the thing—Duluthians don't really give a damn about what's trendy. Folks here just live comfortably and naturally. We don't chase trends. We just do what we do, and when it inevitably becomes big in San Francisco or some such place, we feel embarrassed for the ocean-coast thieves who so sadly try to jack our style.

2000 DEMOCRATIC NATIONAL CONVENTION

It was August 2000, and I had been selected as a delegate to the Democratic National Convention in Los Angeles. It was both the pinnacle of my experience in party politics *and* the start of my growing discontent and distaste for national politics.

Before long, I became acutely aware of how pointless my presence was. I saw firsthand how celebrity, spectacle, and money comprised the engine that powered this machine. A bunch of us attended an extraordinarily expensive party honoring an important congressman. It was hosted by a nuclear-power lobbying group. While we were certainly enjoying ourselves—dancing, eating, laughing—somehow I doubt that the lobbying group was spending all this money for the enjoyment of young, powerless delegates.

Thinking back on that experience, one particular moment stands out. On our way to the arena one afternoon, I was excited to see that Rage Against the Machine was playing a public concert. I loved that band and was excited to catch a glimpse of the show.

But then the truth hit me like a punch to the gut as our shuttle bus navigated behind concrete barriers, barbed wire, and S.W.A.T. police separating the convention hall—the seat of power—from the concert. I realized that as a delegate I was part of the Machine the band was Raging Against.

COMPETENCY IS TRAGICALLY FORGETTABLE

I vaguely remember seeing this really impressive politician on C-SPAN. She focused on policy and presented issues with honesty and with facts. I wish I could remember her name. She seemed pretty sharp. Dang; what was her name? She was amazing!—presented super thoughtful solutions to our country's most pressing problems. Totally unlike all those famous and obnoxious politicians. We definitely need more leaders like … like … oh cripes, what *was* her name?

SEPTEMBER 11, 2001

It was primary election day. City council and school board seats were on the ballot. Even though everything was very low-key, and polling places were quiet, I thought it was odd and inappropriate that polling judges were listening to Minnesota Public Radio. Then I heard the news—a plane had hit the World Trade Center.

The ripples of that day and its tragic events will never stop expanding outward. They are a permanent part of our history and our shared understanding of the world. We immediately became nostalgic for life before the attacks, and some of us, in our sadness, grief, and confusion, wanted vengeance.

Our nation's political overreaction felt like a sign of weakness and retreat. Before that day, America's greatness had been an outward-facing confidence in the founding principles—a belief that the untamed, uncultivated principle of freedom held more power and influence than regimes based on random violence.

Our frantic call for retribution found justification for war. The nation chose to limit our own freedoms. We got sucked into a traditional ground game against a group of fanatics who had nothing to lose and everything to gain in going head-to-head with the world's only superpower.

The dangers were real, and our feelings of vulnerability were justified. Yet, it's also true that our own demands for reaction clouded our judgment. Politicians couldn't keep themselves from pandering to the emotions of the moment via overreaction. For years, the most powerful and influential country in the world governed from a position of fear.

BE CAREFUL WHAT YOU VOTE FOR

There is a jarring disconnect between the characteristics we have been taught to seek in our candidates and our expectations for their performance in office. During campaigns, we celebrate candidates who are "tough" and "aggressive" and "ready to fight," while we brand thoughtful, policy-minded candidates as "passive" and "boring." During times of supposed governance, we bemoan legislative bodies as they devolve into dysfunction, while we yearn for sound leadership.

Should we be surprised when …

> » the aggressively ambitious candidate
>   sacrifices the common good for personal advancement?

> » the supremely confident candidate
>   turns out to be strident and vain?

> » the uncommonly persuasive candidate
>   uses those same talents to mislead and distract?

> » the rigidly principled candidate
>   serves as a partisan warrior at the expense of progress?

> » the brutally honest candidate
>   becomes the brutish politician?

In essence, we've been conditioned to seek and reward the very characteristics that result in a single-digit approval rating for Congress.

Campaign • In Office
We want a FIGHTER
Defeat THE other guys
VOTE
I FIGHT for you
STOP FIGHTING FIX PROBLEMS!
WE WANT COMPROMISE
I FIGHT for you

CHRISTIANITY IS NOT A MONOLITH

A newspaper op-ed I wrote in the aftermath of the 2004 presidential elections:

A friend of mine was bemoaning the result of the recent elections. He is a sincere type, a good family man, who had worked hard for Senator Kerry—made phone calls, knocked on doors—this was the most important election in his lifetime and he wasn't about to sit on the sidelines. While debriefing after Election Day, he stated, "Christians sure are loyal to the Republican Party."

I bristled at this suggestion. "Not THIS Christian." And I went on a brief tirade letting out my frustration toward the idea that President Bush won on the "morality" vote.

Of course, I wasn't surprised that my friend drew this conclusion—it's a simple way to summarize a complex election. This idea is nothing new, and it has created its own self-fulfilling prophecy. If we accept the assertion that people of strong faith vote Republican, then a person of faith would almost feel compelled to conform to this rule and also vote Republican in order to fit the profile of a good Christian.

But that is simply not the case. There are millions of progressive Christians who believe as strongly in their faith as they do about the role of government to help those in need, who believe as strongly in Christian values of love, forgiveness, and the teachings of Jesus as they do about the principle of separation of church and state. We do ourselves and our country a great disservice when opinion leaders suggest that Christians cannot be good Democrats and that Democrats cannot be good Christians.

I grew up as a preacher's son—my Dad's church was a charismatic, non-denominational Christian Fellowship. Today it would be known as an Evangelical congregation, but it did not follow the model that is so prevalent today. Like many PKs (preacher's kids), I've struggled to find my own spiritual path and identity apart from my parents—but I am a person of strong faith, and I have my parents to thank for that. I thank them for introducing me to a God of love, of forgiveness, of sacrifice, and a God who is most interested in a relationship with me and my personal salvation, rather than in the judgment of others.

I know there are many kind, generous, loving Christians who span the political spectrum—from the most liberal to the most conservative, and most will point to their faith as the source of their ideology. Christianity is not a monolith. It is not one size fits all, and it is certainly not (or should not be) the political base of one party or the other. The insistence of a secular Democratic party versus a Christian Republican party is not only false in its simplicity, it is a dangerous assertion that devalues the complexity of faith, ideology, and each person's journey for truth and understanding.

MAKING HEADWAY

Cynicism doesn't solve problems, but cynics are great at calling attention to what's wrong. Idealism also doesn't solve problems, but idealists are great at philosophizing about the world as we'd like to see it. Seems like if we could convince cynics to see possibilities and idealists to make tough choices, we might have real opportunity to make headway.

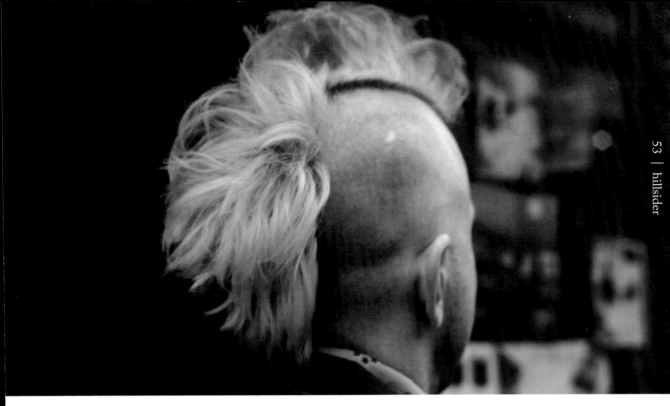

RAWK AND/OR ROLL

After college, my school-structured community of athletes and student-government nerds dispersed into adult life. I felt alone and adrift. I had no idea where I fit in or how to figure it out.

I eventually found a sense of belonging in an emerging local music scene. Most of us were twentysomethings who'd come of age during the grunge era. We created community in smoky clubs, gripping beers and watching bands of our peers play loud, original rock tunes.

That early version of the scene was full of creative, honest, hilarious, entrepreneurial, grounded, ironic, incredibly hard-working, and often self-destructive women and men. The NorShor Theatre was our epicenter. We also hung out at the Red Lion Bar, R.T. Quinlan's Saloon, and any other place where a drum kit and some amps could fit.

I connected with the raw, unvarnished energy that absolutely poured out of the scene's music and people. I loved being the least cool, least interesting person in the room—just a face in the crowd hanging out and appreciating others' talents. It was a perfect antidote to the pretense of political life.

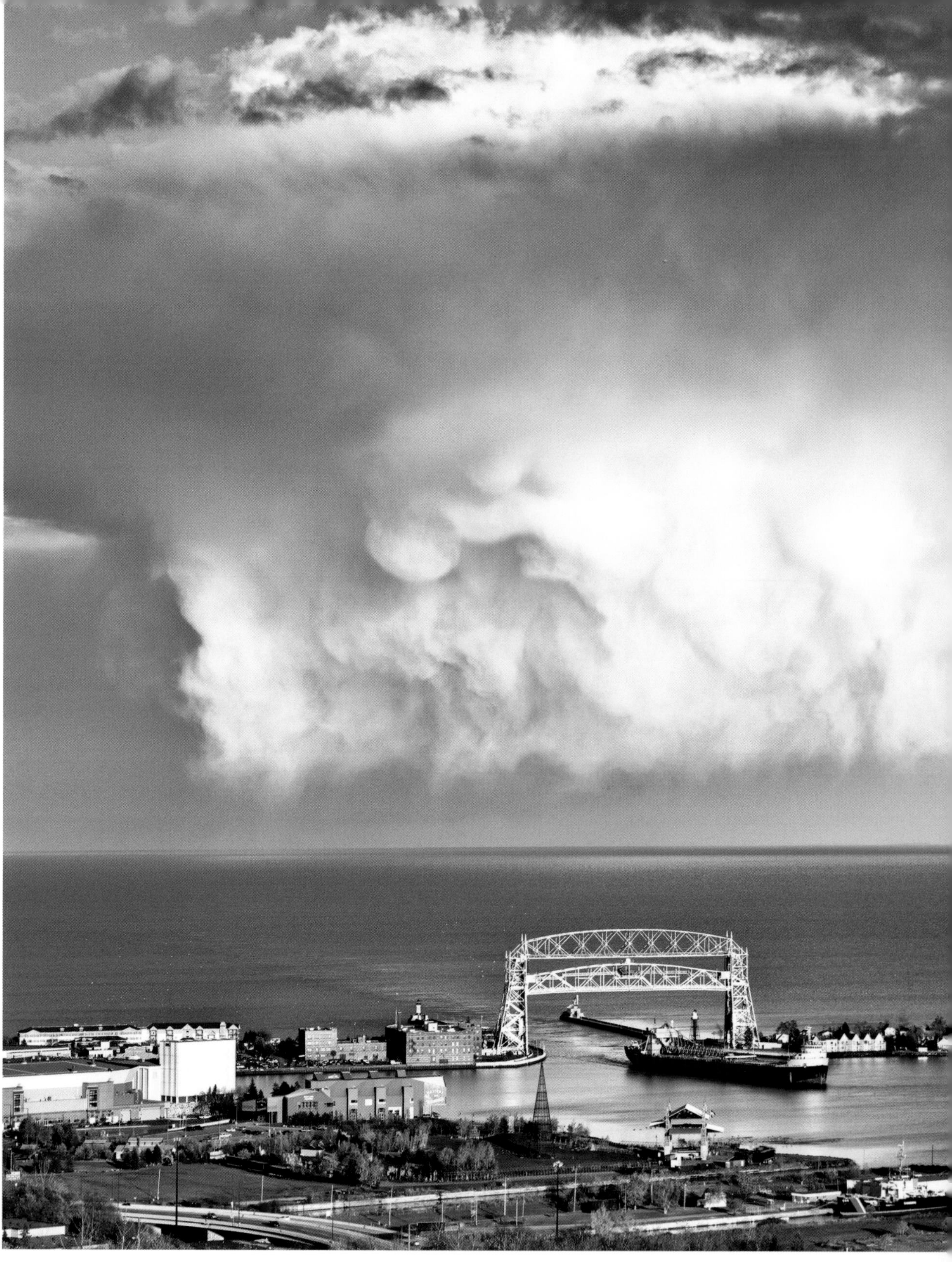

THE HORIZON BELOW

Driving to work, pumping gas, walking to a neighborhood park with my family, my eye is often drawn, unintentionally or perhaps instinctively, down to a distant horizon where ever-changing hues of lake and sky meet.

It's a strange and magical feeling to live with the horizon below your feet.

FLOSSING BENCH

In my late twenties, I lived a quick downhill jaunt from a little corner of Leif Erickson Park that became my place of solitude and contemplation.

On many warm summer nights, I'd follow a short path through a small flower garden (lovingly maintained by community volunteers) to my spot—a small bench surrounded by massive trees that created a lush green canopy. Like many Duluth places, the spot is beautiful on its own but doubly so because of its view. The bench is intentionally angled toward Lake Superior, positioned so the huge tree trunks create a natural frame for passing ore boats.

This was my place of serenity. A place where troubles of the day could ebb away and I could ponder the amazing beauty of where I live. It was the perfect place to sit, to reflect, and, most importantly … to floss my teeth.

Imagine, a perfect flossing spot just two blocks from the back door of my apartment. But only now, as I look back, do I realize how unusual it is to find moments of symbiotic alignment between my oral and spiritual health. I miss those days.

BACHELOR LIFE

Seriously … I *loved* my apartment.

The space itself wasn't anything special. It was long and narrow and had neighbors who bumped heavy-bass dance music late into the night. But its location was amazing—right in the heart of the Plaza neighborhood.

Steps from the back door of my ground floor apartment there was a Video Vision (for 99 cent movie rentals), the Beijing Chinese restaurant (for bliss in a cardboard container), a gas station (for free air for my bike tires), a Jubilee grocery store (for spaghetti noodles), a Little Caesars (for pizza! pizza!), a 24-hour fitness gym (for a shaming presence), a women's consignment store (which wasn't helpful at all), a Hallmark store (for all those times when I forgot to buy a gift), and a 24-7 Walgreen's (for Hot Pockets and Jack's frozen pizza!).

My typical week consisted of significant parts watching Twins baseball, playing basketball at the Y, going to multiple rock shows at smoky clubs, buying CDs I couldn't really afford, and staying up until 1 a.m. every night to catch up on work email and council business.

It was awesome! Right up to the moment it wasn't. Nothing changed except my own perspective. I was ready for something more meaningful … and inconvenient.

My bachelor life at 1220 ½ East First Street, Apartment A, was analogous to a ham and cheese Hot Pocket. It was quick, convenient, and temporarily satisfying. But at some point, I figured out it was really quite awful. I was ready for something a little more real.

COUNCIL APPOINTMENT

Tension filled the Duluth City Council chambers as the city clerk read results of a ballot to decide which of three strong candidates would fill a vacant council seat. Most councilors had voted for the conservative or liberal candidates. The moderate candidate I supported had received two of the eight votes.

The rules stipulated that after five ballots the candidate with the fewest votes would drop off, but that by a majority council vote a dropped candidate could come back for reconsideration. On this night, the moderate candidate had dropped off, and most people in the chamber assumed his supporters would vote for the liberal candidate and give her the victory. It didn't work out that way.

I voted for the conservative candidate, splitting the council into a 4-4 deadlock. I liked and respected him, but my vote was a cynical, dishonest tactic. I wanted the chance to make a motion to reintroduce the moderate candidate. I announced that if the motion to reintroduce failed I would vote for the liberal candidate. Council conservatives supported the motion to reintroduce, the moderate won 5-3 on the next ballot, and we had filled our vacant seat.

In the moment, I felt justified because I had followed the rules and the new councilor had broad support. But I soon regretted and felt embarrassed by my actions. Many people felt hurt and frustrated that I would manipulate the process at the expense of the liberal candidate, who would have made an outstanding city councilor.

My judgment and integrity had failed. I felt like I had fallen away from the idealism that first inspired me to run. It was a public, painful, and important lesson.

CHAMBER VISIT

Throughout the 1990s, a fierce workplace fashion battle was brewing. Defenders of tradition, armed with scorn and judgment, belittled advocates for informality and comfort. The simmering "casual Friday" debate was just the tip of the resentment iceberg.

I had chosen my side, and I was a radical. As a Gen-Xer, I fully embraced the generational preference for denim, extra baggy T-shirts (featuring ironic commentary), and, of course, flannel. Lots of flannel. The grungier, the better.

I vowed to push the limits of decorum so that my less-radical comrades could get away with khakis and golf shirts. I was a zealot for comfort. (The added practical benefit was that I didn't have to buy fancy clothes I couldn't really afford.)

One hot summer day, I took it too far. I was wearing cargo shorts and an old Beastie Boys ringer T-shirt. I had forgotten about a legislative meeting at the Chamber of Commerce. My late, disruptive entrance earned me and my bare knees disapproving glares from twenty professionally (and uncomfortably) dressed business leaders.

After sheepishly sinking into my seat, I kept a low profile until conversation turned to upcoming Duluth lobbying efforts at the State Capitol. I saw an opportunity for redemption by providing detailed analysis of current political dynamics and suggesting a lobbying-strategy shift that the conservatively dressed folks received warmly. I made sure to show up for the next meeting on time and slightly less inappropriately dressed.

DAVID ROSS

Duluth Chamber President David Ross is one of my favorite community leaders. Despite his intimidating stature, David puts people at ease with his cheerful personality and broad smile. His endearing, poetic depictions of Duluth have become iconic and never cease to win smiles at community gatherings.

Our Beloved Community

We are so abundantly fortunate to live and work in this remarkable place—this beloved community.

During the day, it is the Emerald City on the Hill.

At nightfall, it becomes the Shining City on the Hill.

It is the Zenith City, meaning the peak, the pinnacle, the high point.

It is the Port City, located on the shores of the greatest of the Great Lakes.

As for me, I will gladly and proudly remain in this rugged outpost with a cosmopolitan flair, this exceptional community nestled into the emerald hillside along the shores of Gitche Gumee.

—David Ross
February 9, 2015

PAY ATTENTION

Be **aware** and attend to the world and the people around you.

Listen

FOCUS ON OTHERS IN ORDER TO BETTER **UNDERSTAND** THEIR POINTS OF VIEW.

WELCOME

BE INCLUSIVE

Welcome all groups of citizens working for the **GREATER GOOD** of the community.

DON'T GOSSIP

And don't **accept** when others choose to do so.

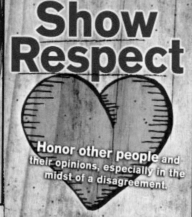

Show Respect

Honor other people and their opinions, especially in the midst of a disagreement.

LOOK FOR **OPPORTUNITIES TO AGREE.** DON'T CONTRADICT JUST TO DO SO.

BE AGREE-ABLE

apologize

Be sincere and repair damaged relationships.

GIVE constructive criticism

WHEN DISAGREEING, STICK TO THE ISSUES AND DON'T MAKE A PERSONAL ATTACK.

Don't shift responsibility and blame onto others; **share** disagreements publicly.

TAKE RESPON-SIBILITY

It's not **what** you say. It's **how** you say it.

Speak your Peace

The **Civility** Project

dsaspeakyourpeace.org

CIVILITY IN POLITICS

The nation, desensitized by hate-talk radio and controversy-baiting cable news commentators, had begun to see governance as a process that functioned something like professional wrestling. As ugly national voices grew more prominent, local political leaders started importing the same tactics. The results were disastrous.

Listserv warriors from all ideological extremes spent entire days engaged in mind-numbing battles of insults and half-truths. Soon, frightened pragmatists checked out and quit politics, unwilling to subject themselves to half-witted bullying by cowards hiding behind fake profile names.

The quest for political influence is fueled by attention, and nothing garners attention like good old-fashioned name-calling. Even when we despise the tactics, our eyes and ears are drawn to conflict and obnoxious voices.

Willingness to say awful things about other people became what is now a well-worn path to political influence. Persuasion via intimidation and fear was an easy way around the difficult work of policy development and finding solutions to complex problems.

Scorched-earth politics was in style. It was awful.

In response to this growing crisis, the Duluth Superior Area Community Foundation began "The Civility Project." The campaign succeeded in the effort to protect and strengthen the voices of citizens who just wanted to be heard. When respectful rhetoric is the norm, uncivil words feel strikingly abrasive, out of place, and ultimately irrelevant.

Incivility still turns up in Duluth politics, but those moments are now outliers. Belligerence is no longer accepted as a normal part of local discourse. As a result, our community debate is healthier—participatory, vigorous, and constructive.

We don't always agree—and we shouldn't—but when we disagree it's most often with the shared knowledge that we're all trying to find what's best for Duluth, and we're not willing to dehumanize each other in order to see whose voice can be the loudest.

MINE

Shortly after running for city council, I developed what I will coin (and self-diagnose as) the Myopic Interest Narcissism Eye (MINE). Essentially, it's the almost supernatural ability to quickly scan large sections of text to find your own name.

Everyone has a bit of MINE, but politicians are professional narcissists and have a sense of MINE so refined that modest people simply cannot comprehend it. It's sort of like a biological Google search function. My MINE is now so acute that I am able to pick up the Sunday paper and through osmosis determine how many times (if any) my name is mentioned.

It's a handy tool. I mean, what appears to be a boring policy article immediately becomes a Most Interesting Article with even just a passing mention of my name.

But MINE is not perfect—it can easily get tripped up by words and phrases that have a similar shape. When my friend Dan Neff was first opening his art glass store downtown, my MINE was consistently drawn to those stories. This was fine, because I like reading about Dan. But not as much as I like reading about *myself!*

One particular phrase always confuses my MINE: "Don't Mess with Texas." Why should no one Ness with Texas? What does Nessing with Texas even look like? I mean, that could be dangerous, right? This statement is really kind of a warning. It's stating quite explicitly to *not* Ness with Texas. It doesn't say what will happen if you do Ness with that state. But it's Texas—it can't be good.

Either way, I've got a problem. MINE is unhealthy. I need proNessional help.

A singular experience. Duluth.

CONTRAST WITHOUT CONTEXT

Consider the following two images. The top one captures the infinite vibrancy of real human lives. The other one reduces beauty and complexity into starkly contrasting abstractions.

Contrast without context defines modern politics. We oversimplify reality so it's easy to describe and fit into ideological molds. We reward politicians who do the same thing.

What if we approached politics with the same curiosity, creativity, and a commitment to advancement we devote to science, art, literature, technology, craft brewing, and almost every other humanity-defining pursuit? We might actually solve some problems. 🛏

ALONE IN BOSTON

In early December 2000, after a full day in a generic Boston convention center, I skipped out on the dinner to wander around downtown. Light, puffy snowflakes lingered effortlessly as if held aloft by the city's ambient light.

I wandered for hours, until I found myself at an upscale lounge designed to celebrate beautified urbanistas. I was completely out of my element. Unfortunately, the realization arrived at the same time as my freshly poured (and hysterically overpriced) tap beer. Instead of looking my pathetically misplaced part, I decided to keep myself occupied. I grabbed a pen and a napkin (advertising Salem cigarettes) and began to write.

I wrote to a woman I had not yet met.

> *12-6-00*
>
> *I sit at the bar of an all too trendy bar in downtown Boston. Everyone here is pretending. They are very attractive and cool and move with a sophistication well beyond their years. And here I sit, in my cheap sport coat trying to play that game. I am sad because I know you are out there and I am certain you are not here.*
>
> *Tonight, I feel like I will never meet you and I am doomed to an incomplete life. But beyond this temporary despair, I hold true to the dream that I will have the fortune to meet you and the foresight to pursue you.*
>
> *I close my eyes and I can see you smile and it warms my heart. Through that smile I can see your soul, your kind heart, your sharp mind, your spirit that lights up any room.*
>
> *You are my reason … I know without you I am so much less. I love you.*
>
> *Donny*

As it turned out, I was writing to a woman I would meet for the first time 18 months later.

"A PATCH OF OLD SNOW"

by Louis Jenkins

Here's a patch of snow nestled in the roots of a spruce tree. A spot the sun never touches. Mid-May and there's still snow in the woods. It's startling to come upon this old snow on such a warm day. The record of another time. It's like coming across a forgotten photograph of yourself. The stylish clothes of the period look silly now. And your haircut! Awful. You were young, wasteful, selfish, completely mistaken and, probably, no less aware than today.

from Before You Know It, *Will o' the Wisp Books © 2009*

PAUL WELLSTONE

Paul Wellstone was unlike all other United States senators. He was a whirlwind of passion, generosity, and incorruptible conscience. He was somehow simultaneously exceptional and utterly approachable.

He represented real people, not powerful interests. He acted to help others, not his own political standing. One of his first Senate votes, in 1991, opposed military action in the Persian Gulf. One of his last, in 2002, opposed the war in Iraq.

Paul's 2002 reelection campaign, a run against former St. Paul Mayor Norm Coleman, held national significance. The country was still recovering from the trauma of 9-11. The emotional tenor of the political debate was defined by equal parts fear and anger as the nation debated a rush to war and

considered imposing limitations on our own civil liberties. Paul's outspoken opposition to attacking Iraq made him a target of the Bush administration and conservative groups who poured millions into the race hoping to unseat him.

Early polls showed the race as a dead heat. George W. Bush was enjoying the height of his popularity, and national pundits were predicting a Republican sweep. That Paul kept his race with Coleman close was a testament to his personal popularity in Minnesota. The real strength of his campaign was his grassroots field operation—the best in the nation.

In early summer 2002, the Duluth field campaign was just gaining steam.

TRAGEDY

The state's political eyes were fixed on Duluth. With only eleven days until the election, Senator Paul Wellstone was set to debate challenger Norm Coleman in what seemed like Coleman's last chance to counteract Wellstone's growing lead in the polls. I thought nothing of it when Amy Rutledge from a local TV station called my cell phone that morning, but the significance of her question struck panic in my heart and sent me sprinting up Third Avenue West to the campaign office on First Street.

My office phone rang as if it knew I had just burst through the door. I grabbed it, winded and uneasy. It was Bill Richard, Congressman Oberstar's chief of staff. He had just received official word that the plane carrying Senator Wellstone, his wife Sheila, daughter Marcia, campaign workers Tom Lapic, Mary McEvoy, and Will McLaughlin, and pilots Richard Conroy and Michael Guess had crashed. There were likely no survivors. I slumped in my chair, unable to speak or catch my breath. The dark, wood-paneled walls closed in, and I sat paralyzed by the enormity of the news.

A burst of excited laughter from the office next door broke my trance. There was a buzz in the office that morning I hadn't felt for months. Wellstone staff and key volunteers were giddy with excitement

Wellstone!

to see Paul and Sheila that night. They needed to hear another rousing Wellstone speech to fuel their efforts in the campaign's last ten days. Campaign work can be grueling, and, despite their dedication, they needed a boost of inspiration.

Now I had to walk into that room and tell them—those people who loved the man and were working their hearts out for him—that Paul Wellstone was probably dead.

We all loved Paul and Sheila. Excitement gave way to a crushing wave of confusion, grief, and disbelief. High spirits bent under the weight of tragedy. We tried to comfort each other while individually processing what had happened. We cried for a while, then eventually we settled into solemn stares and exhausted resignation.

In a narrow hallway of the campaign office, I came face-to-face with a Wellstone staffer. We gave each other a long, sad hug. There, in that swirl of tragedy, sorrow, and uncertainty, I was embracing my future wife for the first time.

LAURA

Laura Scheu packed her belongings into a rusty Jeep Cherokee, preparing for her move back home to Houston, Minnesota—five hours from Duluth in the very southeast corner of the state.

In those tragic days after Paul Wellstone died, through shared grief, we formed a connection that sparked an unexpressed interest. Just hours after we'd parted as friends, Laura called my cell phone, and we decided to meet in Minneapolis. After a long, heartfelt conversation, we parted as something more.

We spent the winter getting to know one another, emailing at least once a day. These were long, in-depth, thoughtful messages. She wrote about growing up in the woods with her four siblings in a home her dad built. She wrote about her rural childhood and about attending Luther College in Decorah, Iowa, just an hour south. Through her written messages, I sensed Laura's generous heart, sharp mind, and kind spirit.

During that long winter of email correspondence, I often thought back to that cold, lonesome night in Boston, when I wondered if I would ever meet the right person. I became certain Laura was the one I had been writing to that night.

Mark Winson, Gary Doty, Donny Ness, Jim Stauber, Herb Bergson

CROSSING PATHS

This picture features three Duluth mayors, a chief administrative officer (CAO) for those three mayors, and a city councilor who served twelve years spanning all three administrations. There is a lot of history among the five men in this photo. Here are the highlights:

» Bergson ends his term as mayor of Superior and moves to Duluth to challenge Doty (1995)

» Doty defeats Bergson in a race for mayor (1995)

» Ness defeats Bergson in at-large council race (1999)

» Doty hires Winson as CAO (2000)

» Stauber and Bergson elected in at-large council race (2001)

» Bergson defeats Stauber in mayoral primary (2003)

» Stauber supports Bergson in successful mayoral general election (2003)

» Bergson retains Winson as CAO after his inauguration (2004)

» Stauber turns quickly against Bergson, becoming chief adversary (2004)

» Bergson fires Winson as CAO by taping a note to his office door (2005)

» Ness defeats Bergson in mayoral primary with Stauber support (2007)

» Stauber turns quickly against Ness, becoming chief adversary (2008)

» Ness hires Winson as CAO, but Winson's heart isn't in it, and he resigns two months later (2009)

» None of these guys holds any city position (2016)

Thoughtful politicians inevitably come to realize how unimportant they are in most people's day-to-day lives.

What if…? Nah. Nevermind.

Go ahead, what's on your mind?

What if we trusted the American public's intelligence and intuition? What if we spoke to them honestly about the scope of our challenges and the uncomfortable, unpopular choices necessary for solving our problems? What if we trust them to understand that our tough choices show we respect them, to appreciate our courage in making those choices, and to show appreciation by always supporting our causes and candidates? What if during tough times we connected with folks' intelligence and courage instead of their weakness and fear?

Ha! That's sweet. Oh kid, you've got so much to learn about politics.

perfect**uluth**day

perfect**uluth**day

perfect**uluth**day

perfect**uluth**day

⊥ɔǝɟɹǝduluthday

The name itself is a celebration: Perfect Duluth Day. A community website like no other, PDD (as the acronym-inclined call it) started in 2003 as a simple blog dedicated to highlighting Duluth culture. Within a few years, the number of contributors reached into the hundreds, and commenters into the thousands. The website expanded in 2011 to include the PDD Calendar, a daily rundown of events in the region.

Reading PDD is like having a Pizza Lucé brunch-and-Bloody-Mary date with a sweet, approachable local barista or bartender who can keep up an endless patter of Duluth-scene trivia. She may seem superficial, but there's a mysterious glint in the eyes behind those retro horn-rimmed glasses. She and her stories are impossible to interpret. Is she ironic or sincere? That's the PDD experience.

"We have a lot of important roles to fill at PDD. People depend on us for details about all the stilt-walking classes, casket-shop openings, Bunco tournaments, ukulele carnivals, masquerade cakewalks, roller derbies, and tamarack dances happening in our region. They need advice on how to deal with ticks, ice dams, tent caterpillars and cracked sidewalks. They need recommendations on snowmobile mechanics and finding a good cup of egg coffee. They need a place to ridicule the misused possessive apostrophes on the awnings of local businesses. The responsibility is overwhelming. It keeps me awake at night."

—Paul Lundgren, president, Perfect Duluth Day

DONNY TO DON

During my first council term, every issue felt loaded with political consequences. My naïveté and inexperience had led to painful public lessons and invaluable experience.

I emerged from that wringer with a stronger voice and a thicker skin. Entering into my reelection campaign, I felt like the local political game was slowing down. No longer reacting, I could filter out the noise and focus on important issues. The milestone age of thirty was in sight, and my council and community presence was evolving.

But public perception of me was stuck. People knew me as Donny, the kid councilor. Boyish, inspired, wobbly legged—I had shared my public (and often awkward) growing process with the entire community. The adolescent nickname fit, and I accepted the assumptions (both positive and negative) that came with it, because it was an honest indication of my experience. Until it wasn't.

Eventually the label felt constricting. I outgrew it. I thought I should shed it before I was stuck with it for good. Like a childhood actor who gets trapped by their little-kid persona, I was in danger of forever being typecast as Kid Councilor Donny Ness. If I wanted to start the next chapter of my life I'd have to scrap the boyish label.

I let it be known that from now on I was Don instead of Donny.

People just loved that decision.

"We're with you, Donny!" they'd say.

Section II

In which a young man looks up the
word "tribulation" in the dictionary.

Ages 30–35 | 2005–2010

GROWING DISCOURAGEMENT

As a college student, I found it fascinating to watch political types practice their craft. They always seemed to know exactly what they were doing, and I naïvely revered their political judgment, bold conduct, and professed mastery of campaign gamesmanship. Then at some point it occurred to me: much of what they were doing and saying was not only wrong, but bad for the country.

Thus began a long, heartbreaking journey toward confronting the brokenness of our political system—toward realizing that so much of politics is just aggressive theater, blunt-force tactics designed to bolster narrow self-interests, and embarrassing displays of power that emphasize rhetorical weaponry over process.

Most disappointing, there was no real thought in the system. It was almost entirely action and reaction. I developed a real contempt for this type of transactional politics driven largely by personality conflicts and trivial grievances. Where was the system described in my seventh-grade civics class?

Years after that epiphany about lack of substance, my own political life had started to feel burdensome and, at times, pointless. What was I even doing? My contempt for political realities far exceeded my influence. In my most honest moments, I had to admit I wasn't changing anything.

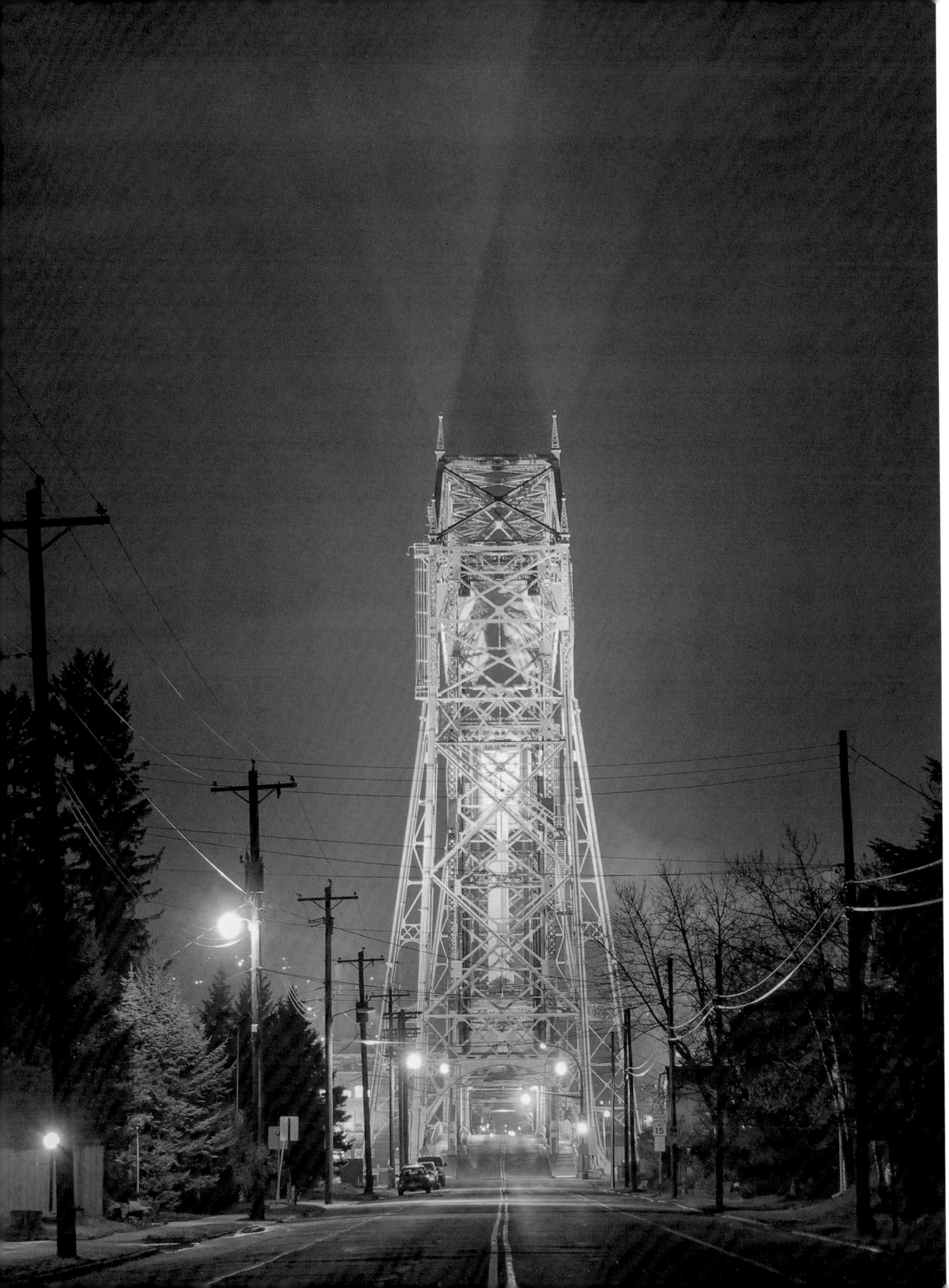

OUR WEDDING

As a kid, even in college, I always felt more like a witness to than a participant in my friends' antics. They enjoyed their youth while I took in their hijinks—watched, smiled, laughed—from a bystander's distance.

I also had a sense that as I aged I'd find opportunities to stop just observing (fewer keg parties) and start participating (more boring policy meetings!). Approaching thirty felt like a chance to shed my youthful bachelor habits and embrace life as a fully-formed, adult, human male.

Laura moved back to Duluth that April 2003 and got a job building houses for Women in Construction. We were engaged that summer (I loved telling people my fiancée was a construction

worker), we opened a vintage clothing store in October, and I was campaigning for the November election. That winter I turned thirty, started my second council term, and hitched my wagon to an amazing woman. A month after the wedding, we learned our first child was on the way.

I still marvel at how gracefully Laura transitioned from southeastern Minnesota country life to very public city life. I can't imagine a better life partner. The most exciting part of that time for me was making lifelong commitments as a husband and a father—finally building something made to last.

PRO-FAIL TACTICS

Let's say two senators connect over a mutual idea and choose to consummate an initiative that could result in the creation of solution-focused governance and the Miracle of Legislation.

Then another senator who *hates* the idea of progress comes along. He finds political advantage in establishing predictions of failure very early on because he believes it will give him greater told-you-so currency later on. Plus, he can't have other senators out there accomplishing things, which would make him look terrible in comparison.

His opposition is not circumstantial or random: it's a philosophy, a strategy, a movement. He is one of thousands out there (politicians, lobbyists, commentators) who define themselves by their commitment to failure of the legislative process. Let's call them pro-failureites.

Pro-failureites use powerful, cynical pro-failtactics to frustrate progress and block even the most virtuous legislation. The opposing senator has gathered power and influence by preventing progress. His colleagues know legislation won't move forward unless he decides not to oppose it.

Our idealistic heroes are committed to positive change. They see tremendous potential in their initiative and they commence their advocacy. But the pro-failureite senator using pro-failtactics is relentless: filibuster this, powerful lobbyist that; attack ads here, poison pills there. His efforts ooze with smarmy, ugly, putrid politics.

It is clearly an unfair fight—our heroes need to justify change, to predict the future, to address concerns (both founded and un). The pro-failureite senator has only one unifying and consistent message, tactic, and goal: NO.

Our heroes put in a cheerful effort, they enjoy the challenge, and they believe in their cause. But these days it seems that pro-failtactics are about 99.98 percent effective. These tactics are clearly serving to sterilize political effectiveness to the point that folks have simply stopped trying. It makes me wonder about the future of our democracy. 🛋

PIGEONS

Pigeons, she said—when she called me that night, frustrated and hopeless—were making her life miserable. Her primary income came from running a small daycare out of her home, but a next-door pigeon party was jeopardizing that livelihood.

Her neighbor regularly dumped huge piles of birdseed that attracted all kinds of critters but especially pigeons, which roosted in the neighborhood by the dozens. Pigeons, which show very little respect for property lines, were everywhere. Folks found pigeon poop all over their homes and yards—the caller's daycare kids found so much pigeon poop in her backyard she had to stop letting them play outside. She tried talking to the birdseed neighbor but was rebuffed.

To be honest, I was apprehensive about taking on this issue. Neighborhood conflicts are almost always messy and based on intractable perspectives. But I empathized with the daycare operator's frustration toward having her life so dramatically impacted by a neighbor.

That, in a nutshell, is the joy of city government: everything is personal and immediate. It's not about broad, philosophical debate or ideological battles that span election cycles. It happens on the level of strong, personal connections and ownership.

City government is about direct, tangible opportunities to solve problems and help make people's lives just a little bit better. Not figuring out world problems. Not creating a historic legacy. Just helping people. That's pretty cool.

I did get involved, and in the end, the council passed an ordinance that prohibits bulk bird feeding in residential areas. The neighbor complied, and after a few months, the neighborhood's pigeon population had dropped dramatically. I still see the daycare provider around town. She always thanks me, and I always feel grateful for getting to help. I love local government for stories like that. 🪑

WINTER EVENINGS

In the summer, I miss dark, quiet nights like this one. The entire world is the room you're sitting in. Nothing else exists. It's so quiet and absolutely still that any motion feels significant. Darkness envelops the city. Bitter cold discourages activity, and snow absorbs all remaining ambient noise. The air becomes somehow more substantial, as though silence were tangible enough to feel against your skin. Even the hum and thrum of the city sounds can't get through it. The city feels paused. On nights like this, I cherish the silent expanse between snowflakes that allows me to sit, breathe, think slowly, and disappear into my chair, then into hushed totality, and finally into the city itself.

HOMEGROWN

The vernal equinox means almost nothing in Duluth, where experience tells us winter weather usually lasts through April. Our first sign of spring is the Homegrown Music Festival, held the first week of May. Even though we sometimes still have to bundle up to stay warm and dry between venues, Homegrown is the time when, as Al Sparhawk once put it, "folks are hungry for a let out."

It's our eight-day, two-hundred-band cure for cabin fever.

While most music-festival names focus on genre—Bayfront Blues Festival, Country Jam, Chmielewski International Polka Fest, etc.—Homegrown just accurately lets folks know all the acts are local. There's a little bit of a lot of genres, and that variety can create bizarre style mishmashes every day of the festival. In a single evening, it's possible to bounce from a bar to a coffee shop to a theater and seek transcendence at a Duluth Superior Symphony Orchestra performance, slam around in a mosh pit while Vitamin Death rages, then mellow out to a solo-acoustic set of nature-worshiping folk songs. It's awesome.

Each new Homegrown adds memorable performances and strange antics to the festival's history, but my biggest kick every year is seeing visible joy and satisfaction on so many faces. All week long, people hug each other, hoist glasses of Dave Hoops' specially brewed Homegrown Hempen Ale, and wish each other "Happy Homegrown!" So many artists, volunteers, and organizers roll up their sleeves to keep the festival going, and so many people fill venues every night of the week, it seems like everyone in the city is invested.

Homegrown means more to me than I can adequately describe. In some ways we've grown up together. The first one happened just a few months before I filed to run for city council, as I was figuring out what it meant to find an identity and sustain a life in this struggling city I love.

When Scott "Starfire" Lunt organized that first event—ten bands playing over two nights to celebrate his birthday weekend—he just wanted to share a good time. I'm not sure Starfire anticipated his cool idea for one weekend would become an integral part of Duluth culture and the centerpiece of the city's music scene.

I definitely didn't realize it would become so important to me personally. I mean, on one hand, it's exactly what it's billed as: an eight-day party filled with more beer, live music, and late nights than might be healthy. But it's also a celebration of community. It's a chance to see old friends and be part of a scene that's new and fresh every year.

For me, it's a profound weeklong connection to the life I enjoyed so much in my twenties, and a reminder of how much potential this city and its people contain when we foster opportunities for them to thrive. Homegrown isn't the reason I love Duluth, but it is tangible evidence of the Duluth I love.

RETIREE HEALTH CARE

The preeminent issue facing the city during my service—both as a councilor and as mayor—was the challenge of reforming its retiree health-care benefit in order to avoid municipal bankruptcy.

In 1983, city employees were promised a lifelong retiree health benefit. The plan allowed the city, which was struggling, to stop paying employees for unused sick days in exchange for a commitment to fund benefits in the future. For decades, no money was set aside for those future benefits.

In the '90s, the plan took on a lot more retirees very quickly, double-digit medflation became the norm, and providing retiree health coverage became (by far) the city's fastest-growing expense. As the benefit became tougher to pay for, so did political efforts of people protecting it.

The benefit was unsustainable and creating a serious financial crisis. In 2005, State Auditor Patricia Anderson predicted Duluth's eventual bankruptcy, and the *New York Times* featured Duluth as a city on the brink of catastrophe.

I was drawn to the complex challenges of financial projections, contracts, actuarial studies, legal issues, political problems, and well-organized groups of retirees poised to fight any potential changes. I wanted to engage in something beyond petty politics. I started studying.

During the summer of 2005, I took the first steps in what would be a decade-long journey. First, I worked with The College of St. Scholastica economics Professor Bob Hoffman to conduct detailed research on the issue. Then we established a citizen task force led by former Minnesota Power Chairman Sandy Sandbulte. The group volunteered hundreds of hours studying the issue and crafting recommendations. I believe it was the most important volunteer effort in our city's history.

The task force report confirmed the city would face bankruptcy unless we took dramatic action to reduce costs and plan for future expenses. It was a daunting task with long odds. The city's future hung in the balance. Citizens and key stakeholders (employee unions in particular) would step up to demonstrate courage and leadership. I had finally found how I might be useful to my community. I found my purpose.

ELEANOR

Ella is sensitive and kind, and has a bright and inquisitive mind. Some nights we'll stay up late, discussing topics of shared interest: the lives of the presidents, Greek mythology, market forces, the structures of governing bodies. You know, just the sorts of things ten-year-olds get a kick out of. A voracious reader, Ella will spend hours a day curled up with her books. Now her love of the written word is translating into her own creative writing.

MEANINGFUL DOUBLE EXPOSURE

by Laura Ness

We used to capture moody, black and white pictures with my old 35mm camera. It's kind of a bummer those days have mostly passed, as it sure is a different sort of way to relate to imagery. We didn't take the camera out very often, so we'd have undeveloped rolls of film sitting around for a fairly long time before we got around to bringing them downtown to have them developed.

Once, we took several rolls of film to Duluth Camera Exchange. After we picked them up, we were pretty devastated to find that we'd double exposed one of the rolls with both wedding and baby pictures, ruining most of the photographs. But there was one exception that was so meaningful and poignant that it made the loss of the other photos less painful. You can see on the right side of this photo an image of me getting ready for our wedding ceremony. The picture of baby Ella was taken a year later. Eleanor was born nine months and four days after our wedding day. This picture is all the evidence we need to imagine her spirit with us on that day. A part of me wonders if Ella truly was with us on our wedding day!

GALVANIZING HERITAGE

The Duluth Heritage Sports Center emanates grassroots passion and energy. It's much more than a place for kids to play hockey. It's a shining example of community uniting for a common goal. Over the years, many people volunteered time and talent to make the Heritage Center a reality. They raised funds. They planned, designed, and built the place. They collected artifacts of community pride to adorn its walls.

The project turned tragic origins into community triumph. On a bitter December night in 2004, a devastating fire destroyed Peterson Hockey Arena. Four years later and about half a mile away, the Heritage Center opened alongside Clyde Iron Works restaurant, transforming a rusting brownfield site into a dynamic new local and regional hub of family activity.

Neither the restaurant nor the Heritage Center would have been possible without an unusually successful public-private partnership that helped the project receive a major State of Minnesota economic development award. The restaurant and center combine for a roughly $15,000,000 annual economic impact and have helped spur business development in the Lincoln Park neighborhood.

at the end of the light

there was a tunnel

MAGICAL PROMISES

Politicians in campaign mode often subtly claim they can do magic. They don't come right out and state it, but they strongly imply it by saying they can deliver significant public benefits without requiring people to contribute or sacrifice. Some even assure us they can increase and improve services while also cutting taxes. Incredible. Clearly magical. Or as some candidates put it, "Just a matter of will" (whatever that means).

Don't get me wrong: it's certainly possible to streamline government, cut costs sustainably, and find ways to provide more while spending less. But all those changes require knowledge, prioritization, active resource management, reliance on strengths, and commitment from government employees. They don't just happen because a politician wants them to.

Despite candidates' breezy promises, making challenging changes requires elected officials and citizens to work very hard. It's that simple.

Whenever I see candidates making magical promises, I imagine Tom Hanks' character in *A League of Their Own*, in the famous scene where he yells at a player, "There's no crying in baseball!" But instead of yelling that line at a baseball player, he's yelling with equal exasperation at delusional or dishonest political candidates, and he's saying, "There's no magic in politics!" 🛏

It was a cold, damp evening in late October. Snow had fallen the night before, then melted, leaving everything clammy and wet. The campfire we hoped to glean some light and warmth from was sputtering and failing to catch hold, rendering our desperate tinkering with the miserable twig formation useless.

Twenty Duluth community leaders had traveled to Grand Rapids for a week-long leadership program. Our intention was to craft an exciting and energetic vision for Duluth, but man, it did not start well.

Bickering and posturing had polluted the retreat's first couple days, and I was contributing to the negative energy. I had arrived angry that the city's top administrator, Mark Winson, had been unjustly fired the week before (via a now-infamous note taped to his office door). I felt betrayed by his termination. Many of us had brought Duluth's current turmoil with us all the way up Highway 2.

A small group of us gathered—cold, wet, and miserable—staring at a smoldering pile of twigs and newspaper as it produced more choking smoke than heat or light. We took turns airing grievances and discouragement around the non-fire. Someone said we might as well just head home. It felt like the retreat was doing more harm than good.

Mark Winson was part of this small group. We all wanted him to know how we felt about the injury to him. He had just been fired, yet instead of sounding his indignation, he gave us permission to embrace a hopeful tone. He refocused the discussion on how we might get Duluth back on track.

It was a selfless display of leadership.

Soon the dialogue turned from complaining about the limitations of our circumstances to exploring possibilities and strategizing about the other people we might bring to our cause. Before we knew it

We barely realized amidst our burgeoning energy and sudden effusive outpouring of ideas that the actual fire had finally crackled to life, the heavy oak log giving way to bright orange flames. The center of the campfire glowed like a Lake Superior sunrise, fueled by our intensifying conversation.

The moment was suddenly alive with the realization of a shared vision and a sense of its salient potential. We talked about the future of our city, the opportunity to build a new political environment and a new consensus. We talked about the need to re-engage the frightened pragmatists who had left local politics to the professional activists. We talked about the chance to rebuild pride in our city and how each of us had the chance to drive that change.

Then the conversation took another dramatic turn—one that left me feeling uneasy.

As an enlivened fire roared at our feet, a consensus was forming around a new idea.

They wanted me to run for mayor.

GRANDMA MARGE

Full of spirit and spark, Grandma Marge was a positive presence in our lives. She was born on Christmas Day, 1922, the youngest of eight children born to Norwegian immigrants.

Grandma was always positive despite living a fairly hardscrabble life. She was a child of the Great Depression and was fifteen when her mother died. She was widowed twice—once by addiction, another time by Alzheimer's.

When Laura went into labor on Christmas morning 2006, our baby sharing a birthday with Grandma became an exciting possibility. Grandma's health was failing, but she was sharp and this would mean a lot to her.

Using my keen husbandly instincts, I decided against pressuring Laura into delivering the baby on a timeline. But the clock *was* ticking. This meaningful coincidence had an expiration date.

James was born at 12:06 a.m. on December 26, 2006. We were all joyful and excited to meet the beautiful baby boy, but as I saw our midwife Jana begin filling out the birth report, I scooted across the room to catch her before any ink hit paper.

"Sooooo …," I began, "my Grandma's birthday is on Christmas Day, and it would mean a lot to her if she and the baby shared a birthday, aaand …."

She stared at me with a look that said she knew what I was suggesting and wanted no part of it.

"I mean," I went on, tentatively, "it's just seven minutes. Do you think we might, uh …."

"James," Jana said firmly, "was born at 12:06. That's just what it is."

"Right. Right!" I said, breaking my own trance. "Of course he was. It's just that … I mean … no. No, you're right."

JAMES

James is such a spirited boy. He brings light and joy into our lives and can charm almost anyone with his infectious energy and sweet nature. As he constantly searches for new experiences and naturally fosters relationships, James keeps us moving ever forward. A warm and generous extrovert, he will no doubt live a life of shared adventures, surrounded by loyal friends.

MENTOR MAYORS

When I began to consider running for mayor, I looked for examples of mayors from across the country I might learn from and emulate. I didn't have to look far. I found two of the best right here in Minnesota: Chris Coleman in St. Paul and R.T. Rybak in Minneapolis.

These guys have often been lumped together (as I'm doing here) because of their similarities and common commitment to improve the working relationship between St. Paul and Minneapolis. While their similarities are many and evident, Chris and R.T. contrasted and complemented each other with unique style and tone.

Chris Coleman is a modern Renaissance man. Whether playing guitar in a rock band or leading a revitalization of a once-sleepy downtown, his quiet competency and singular purpose kept complex projects on track. He has a sharp mind and a quick, dry sense of humor that helped him rise to President of the National League of Cities.

R.T. Rybak brings a wellspring of enthusiasm and energy to even the most boring or benign subjects. He finds inspiration in ideas and possibilities. He also clearly sees barriers to progress and is willing to take on the toughest issues. This unique combination of talents helped him lead Minneapolis through an era of improvement that has become the envy of the nation.

Chris and R.T. will long be remembered as two of Minnesota's best mayors of all time. I feel fortunate to count them as friends and mentors, and I used their successes to inspire our efforts here in Duluth.

IRRESPONSIBLE

It was the sort of decision that could transform our lives for better or worse. Laura and I had two little kids, a mortgage from the peak of the market, and essentially no savings.

"Essentially" is an exaggeration. We had no savings. We were just barely hanging on. Something had to give.

How could we talk seriously about a run for mayor? To campaign, I'd have to leave my full-time job with Congressman Oberstar. Laura was at home. I had a line on a part-time job that would pay $20,000 for the year, but could that support a family of four?

Laura had always been willing to step into the unknown, and I loved that about her. This was different, though. We faced serious practical and financial implications. And what if we actually won? Then what?

I have always had the feeling that once I leave politics, it's unlikely I'll ever go back. This was an "up or out" moment. If we didn't run now, there wasn't going to be a next time.

As you might imagine, we went round and round considering the uncertainty of our options from a variety of angles and perspectives. We imagined a conversation that we might have in our seventies. We thought about how we might look back at key choices in our life. Would we regret not running? Would we regret playing it safe?

Laura had a thoughtful, slightly worried look in her eyes and something like a smile when she said, "We should do it." Just like that, hand-in-hand, we jumped. It remains the most irresponsible decision either of us has ever made.

"May your trails be crooked, winding, lonesome, dangerous, leading to the most amazing view."

—Edward Abbey

> *"I present myself as a candidate for those Duluthians who believe Duluth's best days are yet to come."*
>
> —2007 mayoral campaign announcement

MAYORAL POLITICS

Twelve candidates ran for mayor in 2007, including incumbent Herb Bergson. The main strategic question in a campaign with so many opponents was how voter loyalty would split among candidates. Six equally strong candidates had the potential to win such an evenly divided primary, rendering it unpredictable.

The scenario was terrible for me. I had broad but passive support; I lacked the loyal and passionate support that wins primaries. A lot of twentysomethings supported the general idea of me being mayor, but could we count on them to vote in a municipal primary?

We committed to a risky strategy. Instead of micro-targeting likely supporters, we would appeal to all voters. If turnout was low, our opponents' targeted approach would prevail. Our success hinged on strong municipal-primary turnout, which is unheard of in many parts of the U.S. but possible in Duluth.

LAWN SIGN STRATEGY

"Hey! Do you mind if I stick a cheap plastic sign featuring my name in your front yard, and can you keep it there for the next four months?"

Lawn signs always felt like a necessary waste of time. They say so little about a candidate, yet they're unrivaled when it comes to visible demonstration of popular support.

But, what if … what if we made lawn signs without the candidate's name? Now that was an exciting idea! A nameless sign bearing the message, "We Believe in Duluth's Future." A compelling message that's relevant regardless of who is mayor.

My idea was that eventually people would figure out the campaign behind the signs. They'd be moved by the selfless symbolism of that candidate to put the city as a higher priority than his or her own candidacy. It would be so totally righteous.

I pitched the idea to my campaign team. Long, uncomfortable silence. Then a question: "Soooo … you want to spend most of our funds on signs that don't include your name?" And another: "No name? Like … no name … at all? Just … no name."

Put that way, it didn't sound so clever.

Eventually and unfortunately, I relented to convention. My name was front and center on our signs. I felt like such a sell-out. My own name on the lawn sign? Meh.

Every campaign action reveals something about the candidate's leadership, creative thinking, and ability to craft a narrative. The nameless lawn sign idea would have said more about the spirit of the campaign than our 3,000-word brochure said. I regret not going for it. If you're reading this and want to try it, you definitely should. You'll have my respect for exhibiting the nerve I couldn't muster.

WE BELIEVE IN DULUTH'S FUTURE

THE TEAM

More than one hundred volunteers worked on the 2007 campaign, and in nine months of weekend canvassing, they engaged in thousands of conversations, delivered more than 100,000 pieces of literature, and embodied the spirit of our campaign. Those volunteers were our secret weapon.

FACING DESPERATION

Toward the end of a close campaign, inevitable doubt creeps in. Months of hard work and dedication culminate in a migraine-inducing attempt to predict the opponent's intent.

The uncertainty is agonizing. A close outcome is a second-guesser's paradise. Every small slip-up, every missed opportunity, and every little piece of advice that we ignored, no matter how minute, will haunt us. I think most politicians would agree—it's better to lose by a thousand votes than by ten.

Advice in those final days rings frantic. Nerves take over. Everyone tries to plant their "I told you so" flag in the ground—proof they can use, if we lose, to show their unheeded advice would have made the difference. That desperate advice often damages and directly counters the positive tone a campaign has worked very hard to establish. Last-minute tactics become dangerously tempting.

I'd be lying if I said I never considered desperate measures toward the end of that first campaign. Those felt like desperate times.

I've always told myself I'm willing to lose on my own terms, and I ran my campaigns accordingly. But this time, I had a family to think about. Our future was at stake and I had already risked too much. I had asked Laura to sacrifice too much. At this point, I felt a real need to win.

Ultimately, I resisted the temptation. It was a relief to know I was truly willing to lose on my own terms even in the face of regret and significant personal consequences.

It ended up uncomfortably close. We won 52 to 48 percent. Turns out a sincere willingness to lose on our terms allowed us to win on the very same terms.

HANDS ON HIPS

The traditional campaign headshots we had taken were a complete disaster. When I smiled, it looked exactly like a high school grad photo. My serious face made me look constipated instead of stately.

After seeing the original version of this shot from my friend Aaron Molina, we decided to make it our primary campaign photo. It was clearly more casual than the typical campaign image, and we liked that. We wanted it to represent the positive, confident tone we were hoping to strike with the entire campaign. We used it on everything: web sites, posters and brochures.

I also have to admit, it was totally corny. Around that time, a couple friends would mockingly strike the same pose every time they saw me. "Hey Donny!" they'd yell, then replicate the look— vacant stare into space, hands on hips, one hip jutted out at a weird angle.

After the campaign, Barrett Chase put these together.

A THREAT

On a cool, crisp, gorgeous mid-November day about a week after the election, a political activist and former labor official I'd known for years paid me a visit.

"I come here as a friend," he began, "and out of genuine concern for you and your family. I want you to be aware of what happened to Ray Rizzi."

Even though I had only been nine years old when Ray Rizzi was murdered, I knew his story quite well. I also knew the horrendous tragedy loomed darkly over an issue threatening to bankrupt the city, and my visitor's message came across loud and clear: unless I changed my position on reforming the city's retiree health-care plan—unless I came out against reforming the plan—my life might be in danger.

Ray Rizzi was a rising star in the early 1980s—a bright, energetic family man with a passion for public service. After working for the union in his twenties, he became the city's personnel director at thirty-one. Just a year into the job, he signed a letter telling all city retirees their health care benefit would change. A former police officer was so angry after getting the letter, the story goes, that he shot and killed Ray at his home.

My visitor drove his point home: "People are just not rational about this issue. They feel you are attacking their health, their wellbeing. They're angry that you are threatening to take away something they've worked so hard to attain."

He had started by saying he was approaching me as a friend, but now he was coming at me fairly hard. He wanted me to drop the issue I had spent the past three years working on, the issue I campaigned on, and the most important issue of our city's future. I swallowed hard and tried to maintain my composure.

As I struggled to appear unrattled, my mind raced. I knew I was being tested, and my reaction would be critical. Any uncertainty, any quiver, would incite more threats. But what was the right response? Dismissiveness? Righteous indignation? A soft, "Thanks for your concern"?

It was an opportunity to make an eloquent and emotional outburst that would impress my great-grandkids when, at ninety, I regaled them with the tale. But the test caught me off guard. There was so little time to make this a defining moment. I sat in stunned silence, knowing my delay might be interpreted as evidence of uncertainty or other exploitable weaknesses.

I cleared my throat and chose my words carefully: "The very fact that we are having this conversation makes it necessary for me to move forward. If I let a threat impact my position on this issue, I wouldn't deserve to hold this office."

He quickly pointed out that he was *not* making a threat and was offended by the suggestion.

But I knew what I had heard. I understood clearly the intent of his message. In the end, it only strengthened my resolve.

There is probably no more important job of our government than to protect the citizens of our community. We in Duluth are very lucky to have an excellent police chief in Scott Lyons and a well-trained, professional police staff which ensures the quality of life that we enjoy here in our city. The job of policing is an extremely difficult and, at times, dangerous task.

The danger of the job once again became evident in the recent attack of officer Gordon Ramsey. This cowardly act deserves the spite of our community. The police department has made a commitment to our neighborhoods through the successful community policing program in which Ramsey serves as a community police officer for the Central Hillside. I know Ramsey as a well-respected officer and a quality person who has committed himself to making the Central Hillside neighborhood a safer place to live. Every day, he and every other member of the police force risk their lives to protect us. For that, they deserve our respect and our support.

We should be outraged when these thugs decide to take their frustration out on those who work to improve our communities. Law-abiding citizens across the city should send a message that we support our police force and we will not stand by idly and allow a few bad seeds ruin our neighborhoods and threaten our safety.

Donny Ness
Duluth

GORDON RAMSAY

One of the most important relationships for any mayor is with the police chief. A symbiotic partnership between those two leaders will benefit a community invaluably. I feel incredibly grateful for the years I've been able to work with the best police chief in Minnesota, Gordon Ramsay.

Gordon is smart, hardworking, community-minded, and innovative. As you might imagine, the police chief is handed tough situation after tough situation. Gordon's keen sense of compassion and grace never falls short, even in the face of the most difficult challenges.

I first met Gordon when he was a young beat cop and I was a recent college grad attending the Citizen Police Academy. A couple months later, the first letter to the editor I ever wrote was in support of him.

We have followed similar paths. Gordon became Duluth's youngest-ever police chief at age thirty-three. Two years later, I was elected, also at thirty-three. We've both made difficult decisions for the ultimate betterment of our community.

I have full confidence in Gordon and feel truly blessed to have a police chief that I trust. Duluth is without question a better place because he is our top cop.

DARKNESS FALLS

After just a couple days in office, my goal to depersonalize city politics and depoliticize city operations seemed like a pipe dream. Mistrust burdened city hall culture, which was a quagmire of grievances, rumors, personality conflicts, labor-management turf fights, and political assumptions about even the most inconsequential actions.

There existed a bizarre combination of absolute loyalty to the status quo at a policy level and a bitter cynicism toward the inefficiency that was too often the result of an outdated organization.

Making matters worse, I had defeated an incumbent who valued loyalty above all else, and many of his former constituents reciprocated that passion. Still hoping I would fail, many people sought to prove they had been correct in supporting my opponent. My lack of both age and experience fed a whirlwind of judgment. Dysfunction in the city spiraled downward as the whole organization sped toward financial crisis.

Flying blind, I couldn't recognize the difference between a sincere intent to help and a cynical intent to sabotage.

FINANCIAL BODY BLOWS

In my first years as mayor, as the nation's economy went into a tailspin, the city took one massive fiscal body blow after another. We saw devastating, multi-million dollar cuts in state aid, investment earnings, and police and fire amortization aid, and a $6,000,000 annual loss of casino payments.

One day a knock at my office door preceded news that a routine short-term investment was found to be backed by subprime mortgages. That $3,000,000 investment with a ninety-day maturity had no market value. (Two years later, we recovered ninety percent of the value by bringing a lawsuit against the investment firm that sold the investment to us.)

Our financial situation was terrible, but my political situation was worse. During my first two years in office, I was responsible for fixing a persistent multi-million-dollar structural deficit. We had no reserve and no tricks, so I just knuckled down and made a steady stream of incredibly unpopular and painful decisions that caused Duluthians to pay more and receive fewer services.

Here's just a sampling:

Laying off one-hundred-fifty employees. Increasing parking-meter rates. Drastically reducing library hours and park services. Imposing four days of unpaid leave on city employees. Closing a fire hall and shutting down two rigs. Closing Duluth's only community swimming pool. Eliminating grocery-bus and senior-dining services. Reducing or eliminating cash subsidies to Grandma's Marathon, the John Beargrease Sled Dog Marathon, the Public Arts and Sister Cities commissions, the Great Lakes Aquarium, and many other community organizations and events the city had once supported. Raising property taxes. Establishing an extremely unpopular street-light fee. Assessing a monthly ten-dollar sewer surcharge to pay for improvements that would stop sanitary-sewer overflows.

I was forced to explain and defend many decisions I opposed but understood were necessary. We cut staff and programs, and we cut deep. We raised taxes, and they were steep increases.

It was a poor re-election strategy.

EMOTIONAL TOLL

Night after night, I was tossing and turning in bed. I wasn't eating well. Stress and paranoia dominated my emotional state. I was a mess.

There's a lot of old-school, top-down leadership advice out there: never let them see you sweat; always show confidence, especially in making tough decisions; never give opponents an opportunity to attack. This advice encourages leaders to create distance and a sense of invincibility.

During those tough early years, I did the opposite. I exposed as much vulnerability as I could afford. I accepted criticism and invited people to make me the target for their frustrations.

That approach allowed me to connect with folks and show them I could use my own experiences to empathize, as much as possible, with theirs. I wanted people to know I was coming from a place of, "Things aren't going well, and we need to make some collective, painful decisions to change that." My goal was to find alignment and understanding among Duluth's city government and citizens by acknowledging and embodying my emotions as a citizen and as a politician.

I chose to let people know I felt uncomfortable about what I was doing. Instead of acting like I was confident and enthusiastic about my decisions, I acknowledged, expressed regret and remorse about, and took ownership for how my choices were negatively affecting people.

*"Sometimes when I become discouraged, I say to myself,
I should have gone to another city to seek my fortune.
But then I look over these hills and see the natural
beauty of our community, I console myself and
wonder—where in all the wide world could I find
a view like this?"*

—Duluth Mayor Samuel Snively, 1934

SISTER LOIS

I would like to nominate Sister Lois Eckes, OSB, as the patron saint of struggling politicians. She personifies Benedictine values. Every now and then during my darkest and most dire times, when even friends seemed to be creating distance, I would receive a card from her in the mail. Always a long, handwritten note full of grace, love, support, and encouragement, always at the very time I needed it. Sister Lois has tremendous intuition about when people most need God's grace, and she is always there to deliver the good news.

STEVE O'NEIL

Steve O'Neil was Duluth's spiritual center—a great man with a big heart and an Irish twinkle in his eye. He believed in the goodness in every person. He saw potential in every person and every situation. He fought for change because he saw its importance everywhere he looked.

Both Steve and Sister Lois demonstrate a love of Christ and commitment to embodying Him through compassionate action, not judgment. What a gift to humanity.

A HUG

the BUNION

AMERICA'S WORST SOURCE

Area Mayor Seeks Support Through Painful Unpopularity

DULUTH, MN - - Mayor Don Ness Tuesday said a string of painful and unpopular decisions is actually a plan intended to garner Duluthians' political and personal support.

"I have this idea," Ness said, "that if I continuously make decisions that cause massive damage to my popularity, people will eventually realize I'm doing a really good job."

Ness cited a recent streetlight fee, which has garnered regional and national attention for its abject lack of support, as a decision he believes is so unpopular it will convince Duluthians he is a good mayor and a pretty decent guy.

"Look," Ness said, "Making 'popular' decisions that people 'support' and are generally 'happy' about is only one way to get votes and win elections. I think Duluthians are ready for something new. Something they really don't like. Something that hurts, and maybe just doesn't seem very wise no matter how long you think about it."

Asked to elaborate, Ness used an air-travel metaphor: "Most flights from New York to Los Angeles travel west, right? It's just accepted practice. It's 'popular.'"

The mayor made air quotes with his fingers when he said the word "popular."

"What I'm trying to do is put Duluth on a plane in New York, tell everyone we're going to L.A., then tell the pilot to head east."

When he said "east," the mayor's eyes became quite wide, and he paused as if awaiting some sort of response.

"Think about that for a moment," he continued. "I'm going to make a long, crowded, exhausting flight even longer! Everyone's going to absolutely hate it. By the time we get to L.A., I'll be the most popular guy on that plane!"

When told a local brewmaster had referred to his plan as "bass ackwards," Ness said, "Yeah, I get that. It makes absolutely no sense. Which is exactly why I'm doing it."

One Duluth banjo luthier was willing to give the mayor credit: "He's been very efficient at pissing off pretty much everyone in a short amount of time."

Trampled by Turtles and Retribution Gospel Choir, Homegrown 2009

A one-night reclamation of the NorShor spirit.

"I hope you're proud of yourself for the times you've said 'yes,' when all it meant was extra work for you and was seemingly helpful only to somebody else." —Mr. Rogers

FRIENDS & ENEMIES

"The purpose of politics is to reward your friends and punish your enemies."

—Lyndon B. Johnson

Acceptance of Johnson's poisonous, cynical idea as a truism has transformed our government into an expensive, winner-take-all auction for political power and influence. An entire micro-economy has emerged from the idea. Let me put it bluntly: political strategists, lobbyists, industries, consultants, and the media all get filthy rich from the anti-democratic idea that politics is about rewarding people you like and punishing people you dislike.

Johnson's line of reasoning leads rich, powerful people and organizations to treat elections as high-stakes games of risk and reward. They gamble obscene amounts of money on the campaigns of candidates who promise absolute loyalty and protection. They're mortally afraid that if "their" candidates lose, the winners will come after their riches and power, and sometimes that's exactly what happens. They throw around ridiculous amounts of money so they can keep ridiculous amounts of money and the power it buys them. It's no wonder billions are spent on campaigns every two years.

Political fundraising consultants raise millions by breathlessly hyping the dire consequences of every forthcoming election (while always taking a modest ten percent cut). Candidates must be willing to deliver both rewards and punishments in order for the industry to maintain itself long term.

There is a long list of reasons why the federal government is so broken and why the people responsible for leading the country are unable to do it. The risk-reward dynamic is at the top of that list.

Fortunately, big money has not (yet) corrupted local politics. On a very small scale, I've tried to flip the script by challenging my friends to be part of the solution and working with my opponents to apply the best of their ideas to problems we've faced as a community. I hoped to depoliticize decisions and prioritize community interests. Essentially, I just wanted to govern.

RISE UP!

by Brian Barber

IT'S A TYPICAL LAZY DAY IN DULUTH MINNESOTA. WELL-FED TOURISTS ATTRACT EVER BETTER FED SEAGULLS WITH THEIR SNACKS, CREATING A FEATHERED FRENZY IN CANAL PARK.

AMIDST THE CHAOS, NO ONE NOTICES THAT ONE BIRD HAS MUTATED INTO A SUPER-SIZED EATING MACHINE, GOBBLING EVERYTHING IN SIGHT, INCLUDING A **SMALL CHILD**!!!

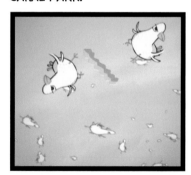

THE GARGANTUAN GULL GOES ON A RAMPAGE, DESTROYING EVERYTHING IN ITS PATH.

CRIES FOR HELP REACH THE AERIAL LIFT BRIDGE ... AND A LONG FORGOTTEN TECHNOLOGY IS AWAKENED.

IN OCTOBER, 1905, THE BRIDGE WAS EQUIPPED WITH CIVIC DEFENSE CAPABILITIES, ALLOWING IT TO SERVE DUAL DUTIES: AS A BRIDGE, AND AS AN *ULTIMATE FIGHTING MACHINE!!!*

BUT THE 100-YEAR OLD TECHNOLOGY IS NO MATCH FOR THE WEIGHT AND POWER CAUSED BY THE FLATULENT FOWL'S STEADY DIET OF MODERN JUNK FOOD.

THE NORMALLY CALM, AMIABLE MAYOR DONNY NESS, IS ENRAGED BY THE THREAT TO HIS BELOVED CITY.

WITH NO TIME TO SPARE, DONNY LOCATES THE BIG RED BUTTON IN HIS OFFICE WHICH WAS INSTALLED SO MANY YEARS AGO WITH THE HOPES THAT IT WOULD NEVER, EVER, EVER, **NEVER**, NEED TO BE PUSHED. ON THIS DARK DULUTH DAY, HE **SLAMS** HIS HAND ON THE BUTTON.

ON A HILLTOP NOT FAR FROM CITY HALL, A RUMBLING STARTS, THEN SMOKE, THEN FLAMES AND ENGER TOWER RISES INTO THE SKY, READY TO DESTROY THE THREAT TO DULUTH.

SENSORS IDENTIFY THE TRASH-EATING TARGET... AND THE THREAT IS ERADICATED

For a special treat, search for the Black-Eyed Snakes' "Rise Up" at vimeo.com.

BENTLEYVILLE

Bentleyville is the largest walk-through holiday light display in the country. It gets local, regional, and national attention for its million-light depictions of Duluth sights (like the Aerial Lift Bridge) and spectacular festive scenes. Add in Santa and Mrs. Claus, cookies, coffee, and apple cider, and now you've got yourself a perfect family outing for brightening up a midwinter night. And it's all free! You can't beat that.

It all started with one guy— Nathan Bentley— decorating his rural-township house and yard for Christmas. Every year he'd add to the exhibit, and before long, people from around the area started driving out to see it. Then, lots of people came. Thousands. Nathan added fire pits for folks to gather, get warm, and roast marshmallows. Santa made appearances. The whole thing kept snowballing until thousands of people were walking through the winter wonderland he'd created. Eventually his neighborhood couldn't accommodate all the interest and traffic.

That's when I got involved. I called him and asked if he'd like to move his Bentleyville Tour of Lights to Bayfront Festival Park in Duluth. He loved the idea, and on November 27, 2009, after six hundred volunteers had worked for ten weeks to get it ready, Duluth's newest holiday tradition lit up Bayfront Park.

You can find me, Laura, the kids, and a quarter-million of our closest friends there every year.

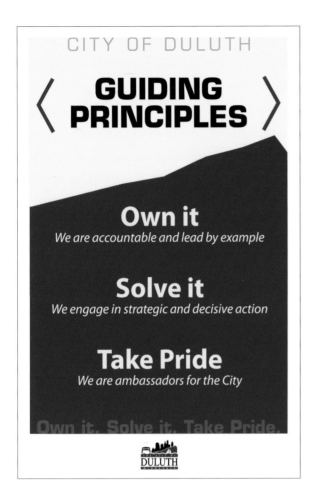

OWN IT. SOLVE IT.

Own it. Solve it. Take pride. When faced with a problem, a divisive issue, or a tough situation, don't point fingers, complain, and pass the buck. Just fix it. Take responsibility, get it done, and move forward.

That's how my staff and I have tackled issues from retiree healthcare to sewer overflows. Owning and solving problems is the best way to feed progress and pave the way for growth. Adopting the motto "Own it. Solve it. Take pride." represented an organization-wide shift in tone and attitude.

Dave Montgomery led our transformation efforts. Plenty of people are qualified to undertake the role of chief administrative officer and manage the organization, but I chose Dave because we wanted to do more than just manage our problems. We wanted to fix them.

We still have big issues to tackle, but transforming the organization—improving the tone and creating the expectation that we deal with the biggest issues directly—has also positively transformed our challenges. A sense of ownership quickly leads to the art and business of problem solving and, maybe even better, taking pride in our workplace.

Own it. Solve it. Take pride. That city motto has become recognizable. Once in a while, someone around town will share a story of a city employee using the slogan while on the job. Those stories strike me. On one hand, they're examples of a simple motto casually used to comment on the value of taking challenges in stride, or to assure someone a job will get done. On the other hand, and most importantly to me, those stories are beacons of a now-organic disposition to take pride in our work—shining examples of important change. I like to imagine the impact our culture of ownership has had so far and what its potential could be if it's continuously cultivated.

INSULTS

"You probably drive a Subaru Outback."

"I have a trophy case you could only dream of."

"From the neck up, you look like the Proctor water tower."

"Your a left wing waco. And you were bad at sports at Central."

"You won. Charlie lost. I guess there are more homosexuals in Duluth than I thought."

"You're probably the sort of guy who comes to a complete stop at the 21st Ave E. yield sign."

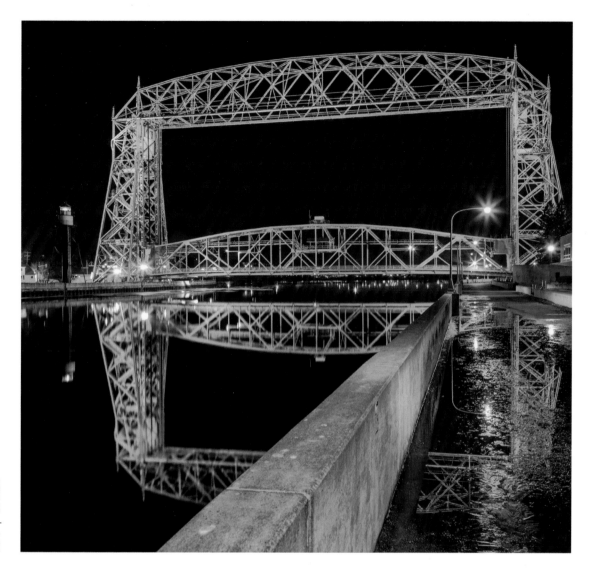

DULUTHIANS LOVE "OL' LIFTY"!

It's a definite unproven fact that the Aerial Lift Bridge is the most photographed bridge between Brooklyn and San Francisco. Hey, that makes a great urban myth! It might even be true. Let's do it! You can help by irresponsibly spreading this idea to others. Remember to state it categorically, with unflagging confidence; that's key to establishing credibility. If they question your statement, you can also say you read it in a book—which is now absolutely true!

#OlLiftyMostPhotographedBridgeBetweenBrooklynandSanFrancisco

CLOONEY & ZELLWEGER

In my first month as mayor, we learned that George Clooney and Renee Zellweger were coming to Duluth to promote their new film *Leatherheads*, which is loosely based on the Duluth Eskimos, a barnstorming NFL team from the 1920s. Wait a minute, did you catch that first part?!? Batman and Bridget Jones were coming to Duluth. C'mon now, that's a big deal!

On the morning of the visit, media from around the region and a number of national entertainment reporters were in Duluth to cover the event. Hundreds of people gathered outside the Depot on a bitter-cold day hoping to catch a glimpse of the celebrities.

I was supposed to give them a welcome gift on behalf of the city and say a few words. All morning, my stomach twisted and contorted with anxiety. A half hour of encouraging self-talk evolved into one simple goal that would carry me through my part. I resolved to not embarrass my city (or myself) on the national stage. Good goal, Donny. Good thinking.

I knew staff had been working on a gift for weeks, hunting down an old-time leather football helmet to display on a handsome wall plaque. Not until the day of the event did I learn they had to improvise a bit because the helmet search hadn't gone so well.

Forty-five minutes before the presentation, there was a knock on my office door. The gift was ready. It was a miniature leather helmet—maybe the size of a tennis ball—placed atop a narrow, cylindrical, wooden pedestal. I was speechless. I couldn't think of an appropriate way to tell staff members I barely knew that there was no way—absolutely no way—I was going to present that thing to George Clooney and Renee Zellweger…

Let's just say my self-preservation instincts kicked in.

I opted instead to present them a customary mayoral proclamation in a stately blue folder. Yes, yes, I know—wholly uninspired. But, on the other hand, I wasn't handing two world-famous celebrities this gift.

Over the years I've reconsidered a lot of choices. This isn't one of 'em.

POTHOLES

Garrison Keillor:	So what is the most controversial issue facing the city?
Don Ness:	*(without hesitation)* Potholes
Duluth Audience:	*(huge laugh of agreement)*

Toward early May, people in Duluth get sick and tired of winter. Then a fresh batch of the bane of Duluthians' existence surfaces in trusty abundance: potholes. Pessimism bomblets. Saw-toothed bottom-feeders pining for fresh tire rubber. Our most persistent epidemic comes at the worst possible time of the year. The little buggers show up in droves as exclamation points on our soggy, dirt-streaked, and weather-beaten winter-recovery season. I think they call it "spring" in other parts of the country.

Ha! "Spring." How cute.

As mayor, I'm a convenient and appropriate target for the frustration folks are feeling.

I could inundate everyone with copious information about pothole formation, freeze-thaw cycles, and the limitations of asphalt patching. While true, these explanations would feel like excuses. Instead, I crack jokes at my own expense and let my frustrated constituents know: I hear you, I understand, and I acknowledge my responsibility. Until January 2016.

"*Even in a time of elephantine vanity and greed, one never has to look far to see the campfires of gentle people.*"

—by *Garrison Keillor from* We Are Still Married: Stories & Letters, *Viking Books © 1989*

OBAMA

When I was asked in December 2007 to be a Minnesota co-chair of Barack Obama's 2008 presidential campaign, he was a long-shot candidate at best. Then in early January, he won the Iowa caucuses, and by early February, when he visited Minneapolis for a rally of 20,000 in Target Center, he'd become a rock-star unlike any presidential candidate since Robert Kennedy in 1968. Some of the biggest names in Minnesota politics graced the stage. I was definately the least recognizable person up there and the only one who had no personal connection to Obama. In fact, I had met him for the first time just ten minutes prior to this event. This was about to become a problem.

(Obama bounds up the stairs to the stage) I can't believe I'm standing here in front of 20,000 people—this is so exciting! There he is! Wow, listen to that crowd! I have goosebumps.

(Hugs and kisses Jane Freeman) She gave a wonderful speech—nice touch for Barack to give her a kiss.

(Big gregarious hug for Rep. Keith Ellison) That's pretty cool—no other presidential candidate could pull that off.

(Hugs Rep. Betty McCullom and kisses her on the cheek) OK, wait a minute. He knows everyone else on this stage except for me. He's letting the crowd know how much he knows and likes these people by these hugs. But I just met him ten minutes ago. OK, Mayor Rybak is next, maybe he'll just shake his hand, that'll take the pressure off.

(Hugs Mayor Rybak even more enthusiastically) Oh, no. This is awful. I'm next. He just hugged all four other people on the stage. What if he only shakes my hand? Or worse, what if he hugs and I'm shaking? Or worse still, what if I go for a hug and he offers his hand for a shake? Or even worse still, what if we do the awkward handshake / hug dance. OMG—what if we have an awkward miss. Dorky mayor, ultra cool candidate for POTUS. Daily Show punchline material!

(Hugs me without incident) Whew. Oh yeah, me and Barack? We're tight like that.

PARENTHOOD

Parenting "gives me all the feels." (I learned that phrase from young people on Twitter. I hope I'm using it right.)

Laura and I haven't had the easiest time of it, but it sure could have been worse. Our kids are sweet. They know we love them, and they love us back.

I'm not going to try to get all poetic about it, because it hasn't been poetry. More like the nonsensical riddles the boys like to ask, "Why did the ice cream cross the road? So it wouldn't melt." Parenthood poetry seems like it might come in two or three decades when reflecting back on the airbrushed memories. Right now, we're still in almost-constant triage mode.

But man, I love these kids, and most of the time I can totally tolerate the exhaustion and frustration that are part of the package deal.

LECTURE ON TAX INCREMENT FINANCING
AND IMPACT TO PROPERTY TAX BASE

"… and so you see, as long as a development truly meets the 'but for' test, the tax increment that is captured by the new development would otherwise not exist. The use of tax increment financing is a tool that allows us to capture the increment and apply it to improvements to public infrastructure related to the development. Once those tax increment expenditures are fully paid for, the taxpayers will benefit by the expansion of the tax base from the development, thereby incrementally reducing everyone's tax bill …."

I went on for another twenty minutes. The crowd was riveted. 🚊

MY PLACE IN AMERICAN HISTORY

Most politicians dream of making the front page of the *New York Times* (as long as they're not in handcuffs). On March 22, 2010, it happened to me. It didn't feel so much like a dream come true.

Above the fold that day was a powerful and historic headline, "House Democrats Claim Votes for Landmark Health Bill," and an iconic photo of Nancy Pelosi, giant gavel in hand, leading thirty House Democrats triumphantly down the steps of the Capitol. Below the fold, only slightly less important, were a story about a U-2 spy plane, and a piece about state tax politics.

There was also a color photo of me emerging from freezing cold water, pale as a ghost, sporting multiple chins and a general look of bodily shock and pain, next to a guy with a dead fish in his mouth.

I mean, c'mon!!! Really?!?!?

My first thought was, "I doubt there is a worse picture they could have run."

But wait! I was wrong. The WORST picture of me they could have run they actually DID run on page A3—all the glory of the front-page shot PLUS a substantial portion of Lake Superior streaming liberally from my nose!

So yeah, that's the time my picture made the front page of the *New York Times*. My place in American history is secure.

At the very depths of my struggles, kind and thoughtful friends would offer the comforting notion that, "This, too, shall pass."

Yeah, but what are we going to do in the meantime?

OBERSTAR VISION

The 2008 elections made Jim Oberstar chairman of the House Transportation Committee. Shortly after, I sat down with him for breakfast. He drew a folded piece of paper from his sport coat and pressed the creases flat. There before us, scribbled out on the back of his official letterhead, was his plan for the future of American transportation. His enthusiasm for the challenge and the opportunity could not be contained.

He was excited to make real and lasting change in our country, put Americans to work, invest in crumbling infrastructure, and ensure our economic competitiveness for decades to come.

The timing was right. The moment was at hand. The economy was in a tailspin, and a serious discussion about a massive economic stimulus bill had already begun. What better stimulus to the American economy than to invest in our crumbling and outdated transportation and utility infrastructure?

But the Obama administration had other plans. They butted heads with Chairman Oberstar. Jim *knew* the importance of this investment. He *knew* the positive impacts it would have on American workers, businesses, and communities. But the administration ignored him. Transportation was a pathetically small percentage of the stimulus bill. The administration promised to reauthorize the transportation bill soon.

But that didn't happen. The administration's attention turned to health care, and transportation was pushed to the bottom of the pile.

First annual Mayor's Bike Ride. Talking here to
Dorian Grilley of the Bicycle Alliance of Minnesota.

FAMILY HIKES

by Laura Ness

Doesn't matter the time of year, my favorite thing to do is hit the hiking trail. From out the front door of our home in the East Hillside, we have easy access to the Superior Hiking Trail and a lot of other paths we've stumbled on and enjoy all year round, although autumn in Duluth is undeniably and truly spectacular. I never tire of taking Chester Creek's trail to Burrito Union or to Jefferson People's House coffee shop. (If you haven't walked down the center of frozen Chester Creek in the coldest part of winter, you haven't yet seen it at its best.) We've covered many miles of trail in and around Duluth, from Jay Cooke State Park to various hikes along the North Shore, and we're always curious to explore the many places we haven't seen. Donny's family has been here for generations; I've been here for 15 years, and one of my favorite things is showing Donny a beautiful place here in the city he hasn't seen before.

Since Duluth is built on a hill, hiking its topography offers plenty of ups-and-downs and a pretty good workout. But those physical challenges pale in comparison to the psychological and strategic challenge of motivating kids—especially during the early parts of a hike—to embrace the experience. Getting them started is always a struggle, but without fail, once we're a hundred yards into the woods, they come alive with excitement and wonder. They seemingly can't stand the idea of going for a hike but love the actual experience (or maybe they just forget to remember to hate it).

The value of a hiking experience in Duluth isn't measured in distance traveled or in the physical challenges one surmounts, but in unexpected moments and subtle gifts. It doesn't take much for me to find my mood transformed on the trail. All that's necessary is being there.

Over and over, Donny, the kids, and I discover a new sense of wonder that a place on the trail can seem so remote even though we're often hiking right in the middle of the city. When the kids find a great climbing tree, we cheer the climb, we cheer the descent, and we bite our tongues when our parasympathetic nervous systems kick into hyperdrive. They gorge on wild berries like little bear cubs. Once in a while, we get lost. One late October afternoon we'd been out in Hartley Park for hours with baby Ella strapped to Donny's chest—it was getting dark and very cold by the time we stumbled out onto … wait for it … the Ridgeview Country Club golf course. We felt totally thankful

and pretty sheepish about having been so close to civilization. We'd started to imagine ourselves sleeping on the trail.

Perhaps you recall what it's like to live through the slow transition from when your small children need to be carried only part of the time, then hardly at all, then—bittersweet and wonderful day(!)—when your back and shoulders can start to fully heal and you are no longer called upon to spare them the final mile of work. To encourage and support that complete transition, we sometimes get creative. If the kids are starting to stall out, we'll play games of hide-and-seek, which is a pretty funny way of keeping them motivated, as it often means pressing our adult bodies behind the spindly poplar trees that line the trails. Soon they'll all be too old to not notice the disparity.

Like many Duluthians, we feel lucky and proud to live in a city that is among the greenest of its size in the nation. What a unique blessing to have these experiences in the middle of the city we call home.

EBB & FLOW

A common fear among folks heavily involved in the early days of Duluth's music scene was that our community might fade away as quickly as it had exploded into existence. From 1997 until 2002, passion and creativity felt like enough to sustain it all. Before long, though, infrastructure to support the art was crumbling. The notion that nothing cool can survive in Duluth's cold cultural wasteland seemed on the verge of validation.

The *Ripsaw News*, an arts-based alternative newspaper that had supported and grown with the scene, was struggling and would eventually fold. The NorShor Theatre, which had hosted hundreds of shows, switched managers a few times, became a strip club for a while, and closed in 2010. All-ages venues that supported new bands struggled to keep the lights on.

But a new wave of musicians emerged, drawing in new audiences at new locations. Charlie Parr, Trampled by Turtles, The Keep Aways, Crew Jones, Teague and Ian Alexy, Haley Bonar, Marc Gartman, Mary Bue, and so many more helped diversify the local sound. Veterans of the scene started forming new bands, like Retribution Gospel Choir, Cars & Trucks, and the Boomchucks. This variety made the music scene accessible to more than just a clique of super-passionate young people.

Pizza Lucé established itself as the downtown epicenter. Beaner's Central anchored West Duluth. Carmody Irish Pub opened a few years later. Rex Bar at Fitger's followed. The scene was no longer a handful of acts playing a single venue, but a bunch of artists at great spots all around town. Instead

of Duluth having one band with an international following, suddenly a good half-dozen of them were actually making a living and touring the globe. Even more were landing slots at large music festivals across the country.

Somehow the authenticity of the original movement carried through as the scene expanded and solidified. A culture had developed that no longer seemed fragile and on the fringe. Seemingly disparate elements—such as a folk singer joining up with a hip-hop duo to form a band called Southwire—just came together like a natural part of the local music evolution, with fans from all sides morphing together.

The music scene has grown to become a key part of Duluth's identity. An ever-growing list of new performers continue to make their mark: Wolf Blood, Red Mountain, Big Wave Dave and the Ripples, Sarah Krueger, the Brothers Burn Mountain. Long may the list go on.

LOST FRIENDSHIPS

There is a cliché that goes something like, "Well, if the friendship can't survive a disagreement, then maybe it wasn't a real friendship to begin with." Yeah, but friendship isn't a binary, on-off sort of deal. It's a spectrum encompassing layers of intimacy, time spent together, and countless other dynamics based on each person's life situation and belief system.

I've seen politics influence and damage friendships. In the face of political disagreement, a great friend becomes a good friend, a good friend becomes a casual friend, a casual friend becomes a person who calls you an idiot on Facebook.

In my years as a city councilor and mayor, various folks have sent me to the unfriendly end of that spectrum really fast for reasons I sometimes know and sometimes don't. I've known and been friendly with some folks for decades and then BANG! they refuse to make eye contact with me at the grocery store. The dynamic always feels strange, but over time I've mostly come to terms with it just being part of the position.

But, man, it feels entirely different when it happens with my pre-political life friends. I take those

friendship losses much more personally, and for a long time I couldn't figure out why.

Recently I think I've figured it out. I've always been afraid that elected life would change who I am, so when an old friend is critical—especially when it's in a personal way—I interpret it as credible evidence that I've changed, and the parts of me that person once valued or appreciated have disappeared.

Of course I *have* changed. I'm a different person today than I was before taking office, and that's natural. I've seen it happen over the years. I don't have the same joy, the same patience, or the same enthusiasm for the idealistic principles that propelled me to run in the first place. Sometimes I feel sad about that.

It's possible those folks I've fallen out of favor with really do think I've become someone they don't want as a friend. It's just as likely that they're making a political statement much like strangers do, but I still feel like that skinny teenaged kid who so dearly valued the opinions of those now-former friends. That stuff was the foundation for my sense of self-worth, and it still feels significant.

PACKER INFILTRATION

I'm not in favor of overly strict standards in our civil service process. We need to broaden the scope of people working for city government, and our outdated testing system gets in the way of diversifying our workforce.

However, I would make an exception to help us reduce (if not eliminate) the possibility of hiring more Packer fans. City hall is crawling with them, wearing that diseased-grass green and the crusty, orangish, sat-out-overnight mustard yellow.

I have to admit, despite their horrendous taste in professional football teams, the employees pictured here are among the best I've worked with. That said, I stand firm in my goal to limit

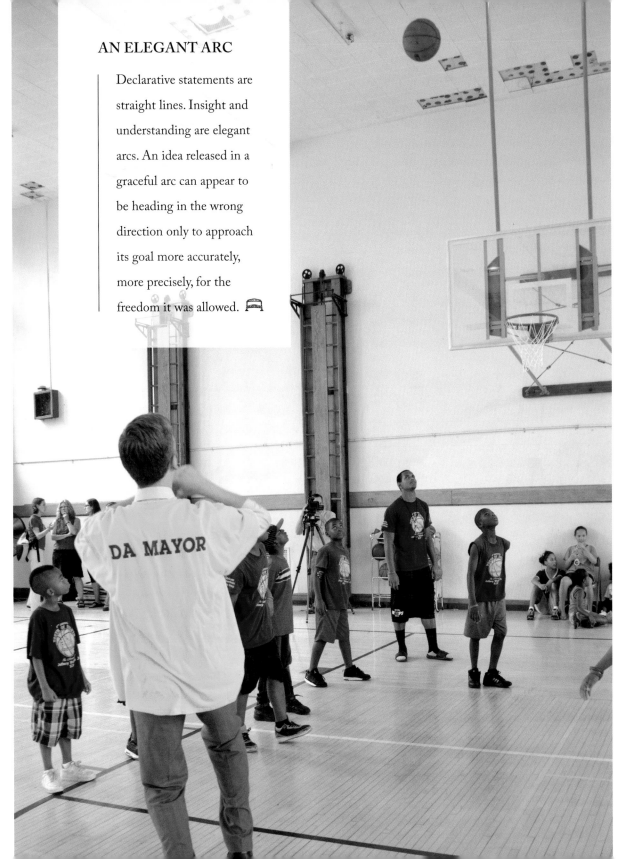

AN ELEGANT ARC

Declarative statements are straight lines. Insight and understanding are elegant arcs. An idea released in a graceful arc can appear to be heading in the wrong direction only to approach its goal more accurately, more precisely, for the freedom it was allowed.

FRIENDLY ALIENS

Duluthians are a mostly friendly lot, but we're not going to make a big show of it. Minnesota nice? Oh, fer sure. You betcha. But maybe a little more grounded, guarded. A little less fuss on the bus. I mean, the last thing we want to do is embarrass our guests by making them feel special.

Here's an example. It's a weird one, but stay with me. Let's pretend a small scout team of friendly, intellectually curious aliens visits Earth. They should definitely visit Duluth before anywhere else. Why? Because they're going to be super on edge, right?, and most other cities would probably make a huge, embarrassing, obnoxious show of it—fancy dinners, special events, promotional t-shirts.

I'm not saying we shouldn't treat them well. I'd definitely use whatever influence I have to get them some nice Holiday Inn rooms, but anything beyond that would just be tacky.

We could show them a bunch of parks, take them to some of our excellent schools, and get them out with some Duluthians who enjoy four-season outdoor adventure within city limits. As we were walking around UMD, I'd point out—but not in a braggy way—the Bulldogs' football and hockey national-championship trophies. I'd be super-casual about it. They'd be impressed by both the hardware and my approach, and then I'd feel awkward because even though that stuff is impressive I wasn't trying to impress anyone and we'd just have to work through that little moment the way Duluthians do, which is to just sort of be silent and look around for a moment before deflecting attention by talking about the weather or something else.

We'd visit Beaner's in West Duluth. I'd probably have them talk to Jason Wussow about coffee and local music. Normally, I'm not all that generous (because some sorts of generosity are really just showing off), but I'd buy coffee (hopefully at a discount) since it's unlikely the aliens would have access to U.S. currency. If they did, I think we'd all be a bit concerned about where and how they acquired it.

Instead of spending our time on extravagances, we'd focus our energy on more practical matters. Like we'd be sure to have a couple of Canadians around to translate our heights and weights into the metric system. Stuff like that. We Duluthians understand it's the little things that matter. As soon as we heard the name of the planetary system they came from, we'd look it up on Wikipedia before

lunch so we could ask them thoughtful and informed questions. You know, to show we're interested in them and not just looking for an opportunity to talk about ourselves.

We'd also look for ways to keep things light and send a signal that earthlings are fun-loving. It'd be funny if we encouraged one of the aliens to jump into the lake head first, then have a photographer snap a picture of its reaction to the freezing-cold water. We'd mount the photo onto a nice plaque for their spaceship. When we presented it, we'd all laugh and laugh and laugh. The alien featured in the picture probably wouldn't think it was quite as funny as the rest of us, but he'd laugh along anyway, having learned a thing or two from us about Minnesota nice.

Cirrus Vision SF50, designed and manufactured in Duluth

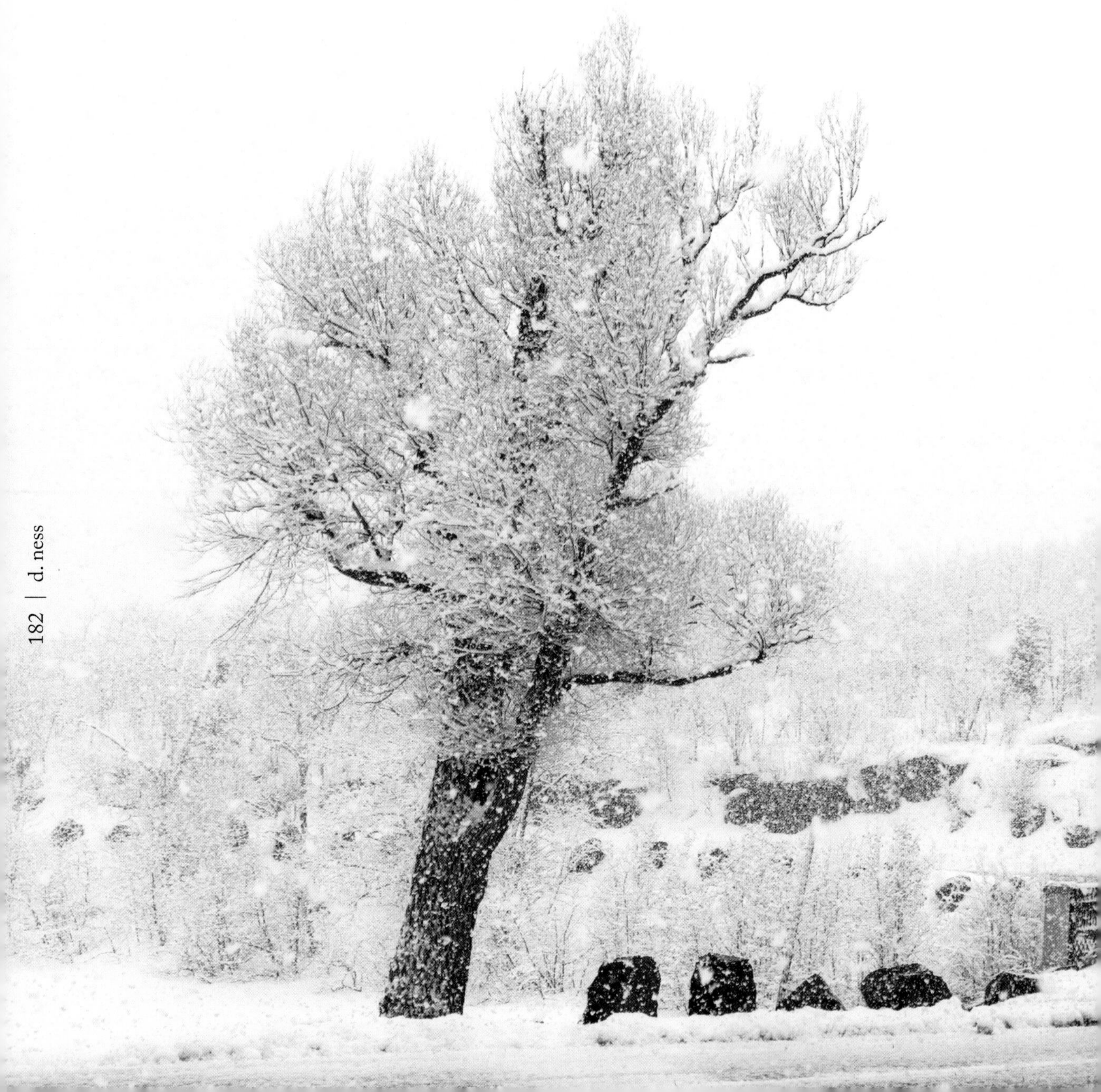

TENSION

The room's angry murmur grew quieter and more intense as I approached the podium.

More than three hundred former city employees—cops, firefighters, and utility workers who hadn't lost their intimidating edge in retirement—did their best to project disgust. They unquestionably saw me as the enemy, and this was the first time they would hear from me face-to-face.

I understood their anger, but I also understood the desperate need for change. I was there to explain why city retirees would have to pay more for their health care. This was my first chance to counter the misinformation and fear tactics that swirled around this issue. I finally had a chance to suggest that inaction was our greatest danger.

My voice shook and my confidence wavered as I began by acknowledging the anger and frustration in the room. But slide by slide, as I showed how our unsustainable financial situation would eventually devastate both the city and the retiree health benefit, my resolve grew stronger. This message had to be delivered—too much was at stake—and these former city employees deserved to hear it directly from me.

I doubt I changed even one mind that afternoon. I doubt those angry, scared retirees felt any better about the financial changes they would face in coming years. But at least they now knew the scope of our challenge and how it motivated my decision.

I didn't want retirees to pay more for health care. I desperately wanted to keep the city from going bankrupt.

I get to do a lot of fun things as mayor. The events
I enjoy most are the ones I can share with my kids.

At this adult spelling bee, Eleanor spelled more words correctly than I did.

ROLLER DAMES

I'm a big fan of the Harbor City Roller Dames. These women are dedicated athletes who combine honed technique and unique style with competitive intensity. The game itself is physical, tactical, and ultimately won by impressive skating skills.

The bouts are an awesome spectacle: DJ spinning dance music; live band as halftime entertainment; brash announcers cracking jokes; brave fans sitting on the concrete floor nervously close to the action. Hundreds gather to cheer the home team. The competitors enter the arena strong, confident, and battle-ready. Best of all, the entire show is designed for the community, and money is raised to support local charities. Go Dames!

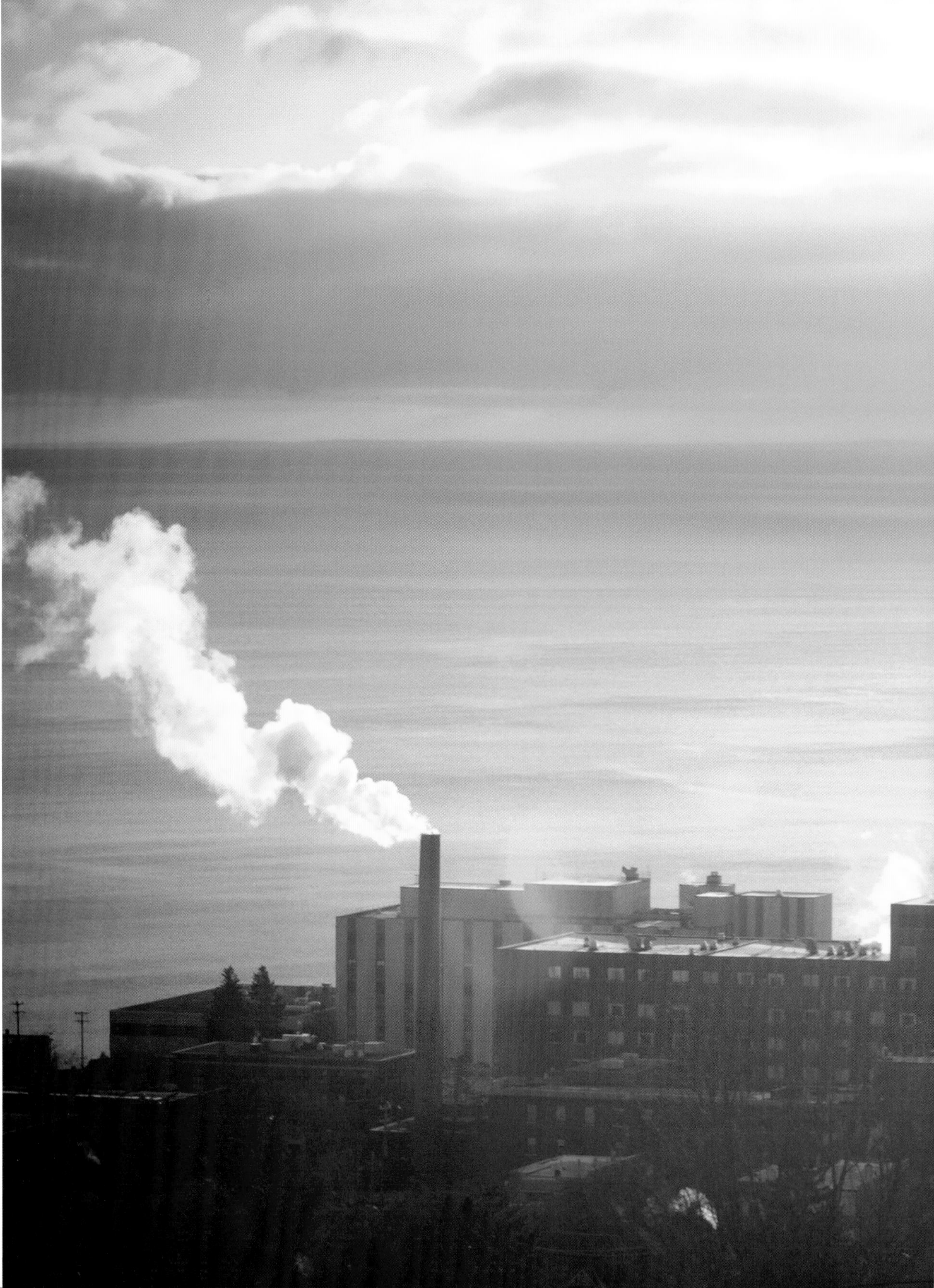

RUN AGAIN?

Congressman Jim Oberstar's 2010 loss to Chip Cravaack hit me hard. My mentor, my boss, and my friend had suffered a painful defeat. We were seeing improvement in city government by 2010, but progress was slow and painful. Navigating through the crisis had beaten me up politically, emotionally, and physically. Laura was pregnant with our third child. We faced another defining decision—was it time to pull the plug on public life?

I was questioning whether everything we were doing was worth the strain.

I convinced myself I wouldn't run for a second term. I saw friends and peers living what seemed like much easier lives than ours: dealing with less stress, working for nimble organizations that embraced their ideas, making a lot more money. At the time, Laura and I were miserable about our role, and for what?

Section III

In which a rapidly aging mayor finally
figures things out, then quits.

Ages 35–40 | 2010-2015

A REDISCOVERED PASSION

I love the work of being mayor: studying policy issues, crafting the city's annual budget, and helping constituents solve problems. The times I feel most discouraged are when I'm pulled away from actually doing that work.

The problem is, the role of mayor invites endless opportunities for distraction: symbolic ideological battles, petty emotional politics, and seductive, ego-driven posturing. Even the fun parts of this job can distract from why I wanted this position in the first place.

As I began preparing for the possibility of not seeking a second term, I focused on issues that I wanted to wrap up during my last year in office. I threw myself at those projects with a single-minded sense of purpose. I engaged with complex details and began finding strategies to move forward. I loved it.

By recommitting to the work of governance, I found renewed focus and resolve. The winds of personality politics kept blowing, but I had no time or patience for what they stirred up. I had too much work to do. I was way too busy to give a rip about what some guy said on talk radio.

I had rediscovered my passion for the job. 🛏

WILCO: HONORARY DULUTH BAND

A dozen hipsters were milling around Pizza Lucé that afternoon, but I (not hip) was the only person to recognize that Jeff Tweedy (!) of the hipster-famous and critically-acclaimed band Wilco had just walked in for a to-go order. I introduced myself and explained I'd see him that night, before the band's show, to present them with a proclamation. He expressed serious doubt as to whether I was old enough to be mayor.

A few hours later, I was backstage at the DECC proclaiming Wilco an honorary Duluth band. They had earned the honor—and thousands of loyal fans—by playing an inspired set during the Great Bayfront Fog Show of 2007. I meant for the proclamation to be a quiet thank-you to a band that had been a personal favorite for a while. Tweedy had other plans.

"This was given by a teenaged boy who claims he's the mayor," Tweedy told the sold-out crowd while holding the oversized blue proclamation folder. "I think it's legit." Throughout the show, he used the folder as a crowd-control device. Anytime he opened it, the crowd would go wild. When he closed it, there was silence. During shows in Madison and Chicago later that week, Tweedy chided those cities for not honoring the band in the same way Duluth had.

Two years later, Wilco was back on a beautiful Duluth evening, headlining another show at Bayfront Park. Throughout the show, Tweedy would quip, "It's good to be home," and claim Duluth citizenship. Then he pointed out that while they were okay with honorary Duluth-band status, what they really wanted was something else.

I was in the audience and sprang to meet Tweedy's new request. After getting a piece of paper and a pen from someone, I drew what he said the band wanted. A couple of large friends carried me toward the stage on their shoulders, and during a long Nels Cline guitar solo, Tweedy stepped to the mic and said, "Here comes the mayor!" I got to the stage and handed him the paper. He read it, held it up, and yelled, "The key to the city!"

IGNORED

One time, I got a thousand teenagers to do the same thing at the same time. All I had to do was give a boring speech at an inconvenient moment. The result? A convention hall full of teens simultaneously ignoring my entire fifteen-minute speech. An avalanche of indifference!

They were high school students who had just endured a full morning of old-splainers old-splaining about jobs and responsibilities and stuff. Now, at lunch time, when it seemed like they might finally have some freedom to hang with their friends, some middle-aged politician was in front of the cafeteria blah blah blathering.

Given the circumstances, I would have ignored me, too.

But there was this one kid. He was off to my right and about three tables back. At one point, he just so briefly, subtly, seemed like he might possibly, maybe, be listening. His blank expression remained mostly just a stare, but a flicker of eye contact indicated possible interest. To this day, I believe he might have noticed I was saying words with my mouth and possibly even heard some of them.

Thank you, kid sitting three tables back! Thank you. I feel like we really connected.

JOHN GAGLIARDI

I was fascinated by St. John's University football coach John Gagliardi's "Winning with No's" philosophy that boldly rejected clichés. He deliberately ignored tools and methods most other coaches rely on: whistles, trash talking, playbooks, scholarships, statistics, tackling in practice, required weight-lifting, and practices longer than ninety minutes.

Here's the best part. By the time he retired, this quiet, modest man who rejected college football's excesses had won more games (489) than any other college football coach.

"Winning with No's" is not traditionally tactical, which is why it *is* a brilliant tactic far beyond a football field. Absence of the unnecessary sends its own message. Avoiding clichés leaves room for substance; setting out to kill clichés can inspire a movement.

At the moment I'm writing this essay, I've been mayor for 2,672 days. That's 64,128 hours. And *still* not a single shark attack on city beaches since I took office. You're welcome, Duluth.

But as the streak grows longer, the burden grows heavier. I mean, just one shark attack (even if it's not fatal—just a little nibble) could devastate my legacy.

It's exactly like baseball legend Cal Ripken Jr.'s streak of consecutive games played. Except in my case, it's truly a matter of life or death. On the day Ripken's streak ended, he just sat there on the bench … doing nothing. Nothing happened. If my streak ends, it'll mostly likely be with violent human flesh-tearing in the grips of a bloodthirsty shark's powerful jaws.

But hey, don't get me wrong. I'm certainly impressed that Cal Ripken played baseball every day.

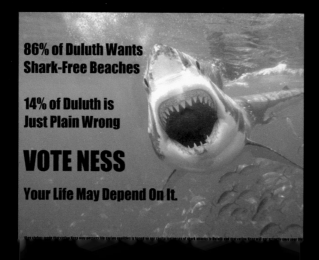

86% of Duluth Wants
Shark-Free Beaches

14% of Duluth is
Just Plain Wrong

VOTE NESS

Your Life May Depend On It.

Keep Duluth Shark-Free
VOTE NESS

Since Don Ness was sworn
in as Mayor in January
2008, there has not been
a single shark attack in
Duluth. Some may say,
"that's just a coincidence."
But when it comes to shark
attacks, are you really
willing to take that chance?

(Any claims made that voting Ness may possess
life-saving qualities is based on per capita
instances of shark attacks in Duluth and that
voting Ness will not actually save your life.)

Actual Ness for Mayor 2011 ads, the imposing truth of which no doubt discouraged others from running against me.

OWEN & THE GIPPER

Owen was born February 6, 2011, a date historically significant for two other reasons: 1. Ronald Reagan had been born a hundred years ago to the day; and 2. The Packers won their fifth Super Bowl.

As a Democrat and a Vikings fan, I could choose to see this as a bad omen. Not me, though. Quite to the contrary. I predict Owen will lead the Vikings to their first Super Bowl victory in 2033, when the game will again fall on his birthday. Then he'll be elected President in 2080, so when he takes office in 2081, he'll be *exactly* the same age, *to the day* (69 years, 349 days), as Reagan was when he was inaugurated 100 years earlier. Think about it. The math works.

Owen was born at 5:05 a.m. According to astro.com, Reagan was born at 4:16 a.m. So, when Owen is sworn in, Reagan will *still* be the oldest President to be sworn in for the first time, but he'd hold that record by just 49 minutes!

Could they delay the swearing in ceremony by an hour to allow Owen the record by 11 minutes? I'm not sure. Probably the fair thing to do would be to time the swearing in to the exact moment so they would truly share the record.

But let's be honest—this is all pretty far-fetched. I mean, the Vikings winning the Super Bowl? I'm optimistic, but I'm not delusional.

OWEN!

It's hard for me to imagine a sweeter little guy than our Owen. His smile is quick and pure, complete with dimples and a twinkle in his eyes. He has a personality to match: curious, sensitive, and funny. He'll be four when this is published, and we can't wait to see who he becomes.

A SPLIT SECOND

Election night in 2011 felt like a milestone. It marked the end of four challenging years of controversy and turmoil. Undeniably, Duluth had turned in a positive direction, and we could feel momentum building. Despite our tough and often unpopular decisions, the community offered generous support, and that night I was reelected without opposition.

I felt relieved and proud for the first time since taking the office. The city I love seemed on the cusp of its next great era. I'm embarrassed to admit I felt very satisfied with myself—gifting myself way too much credit for the good things that were happening.

I drove home around 11:00 p.m. that night, still puffed up with self-congratulation. My twenty-year-old Ford F-150 rattled over dark, bumpy Hillside backstreets.

Suddenly!—a flash of motion flew across my path just a few feet in front of the truck's big grill. It was a bicyclist, oblivious to my rattletrap pickup. I was so stunned that my foot never touched the brake. Eyes wide, fingers clenching the wheel, my stomach twisted as the truck continued its rumbling climb up the avenue, having narrowly missed the cyclist.

I replayed the circumstances in my mind like we all tend to do after a close call. I had the right of way and was traveling under the speed limit, but if there had been an accident, these details wouldn't have mattered.

The bicyclist could have died. A split second could have made the difference between his life and death. A slight increase of pressure on the gas pedal, minutely faster acceleration at the stop light five blocks back, any one of a hundred micro-variables could have resulted in lives forever altered.

A split second.

In an instant, those accomplishments I had been celebrating would have been rendered meaningless.

I couldn't dismiss the moment as luck or good fortune. There was an urgent message in this chain of events, and I couldn't afford to ignore it. On that day, I was in danger of falling into the trap of self-importance and arrogance. I had worked hard to stay humble in the job. But man, when things are going well in public life, it's easy to be blinded. It's tempting to believe the nice things people say.

Nothing is more fleeting than the whims of public sentiment. No sense of self-worth is as frail as one based upon political success, which is not a personal characteristic, cannot define a person, and can disappear, leaving a massive void, in a heartbeat.

That night, I promised myself to stay thankful for the people and blessings in my life. I promised to ground myself in what is truly important. I promised to never base my identity on political success.

GIANT SCISSORS & GOLDEN SHOVELS

Ribbon cuttings and groundbreakings require the most vigorous—sometimes downright dangerous—work-related physical activity for a mayor.

TOOLS OF THE TRADE

One of my most notable physical features is that I have very soft hands. No, I mean embarrassingly soft. Folks who moisturize every day don't have hands as soft as mine. Some of it can be blamed on genetics, but it's mostly from an entire lifetime of avoiding physical labor.

In my profession, this isn't an advantage. Especially when I'm hanging out with the building trades or utility workers. When we shake hands, I can sense their judgment of my pillowy, callous-free palm. I can sense their disdain through my pristine, ultra-sensitive skin.

But being mayor does (occasionally) require (moderate) physical effort (holding or) using (relatively) large (compared to a stapler) tools and (momentarily) wearing a hard hat. It's not much, but you need to ease into these things. With the amount of construction taking place in 2015, I might just get a blister. That would be pretty exciting and impressive (to me and my fellow soft-handed politicians).

NUTS & BOLTS

I come from a family that knows next to nothing about auto repair. It's also a family that only buys used cars, which are driven until they die. This might seem like a bad combination, but it has worked for decades because of one man: Jimmy Gaskill of Jimmy's Nuts & Bolts.

Jimmy is an excellent mechanic. He's smart and hardworking, and he obviously knows his stuff. The chief reason the Ness family holds him in such high regard, however, is that he is fundamentally honest. Jimmy knows how ignorant we are about cars, and he could easily take advantage of our vulnerability. But he doesn't. We share an understanding that he will find the least expensive way to keep our vehicles operating safely, with no oversell. If he says we need to commit to a seemingly expensive fix, we agree, confident that his advice is in our best interests.

That level of trust is what everyone wants from mechanics … and elected officials. We want people who put the needs of others ahead of their own desires for wealth and power. When that level of trust is established, loyalty follows, and everyone wins. If the relationship is polluted by greed, it erodes.

Trust can feel easy when everyone's goals and interests align. Leaders who demonstrate courage and selflessness, or who take on personal challenges by making decisions for the public good, feed our sense of hope. Trust crumbles quickly when goals are misaligned. Leaders who act in self-interest feed our cynicism.

Too many politicians care more about their own interests than about what's important to their communities. They'd rather impose a platform—go through the needless time and expense of replacing the whole engine that drives a political party—than commit to the practical work of keeping communities running smoothly by getting to know how all the parts work together, then making maintenance decisions based on what works for the community, not what benefits them the most. America needs a generation of leaders focused on fixing problems instead of exploiting them. We need politicians who serve as honest mechanics who want to fix things.

"Let's have an outdoor inauguration ceremony on the steps of City Hall. It'll be great - the fresh January air will ensure that no one will fall asleep during my speech!"

"Here's your inaugural ball!"

MAYOR DON NESS

2012 INAUGURATION

Monday, January 9
Noon
Front Steps of City Hall
Reception to follow

Attend Duluth's first ever (and likely the last) outdoor mayoral swearing in ceremony!

New City Councilors will be sworn in that evening (6 p.m.) at Clyde Iron, 2920 W. Michigan Street • Celebration featuring live music starting at 7 p.m.
FREE AND OPEN TO THE PUBLIC

SECOND INAUGURATION

The mayor's inauguration in Duluth is always held on the first Monday following the second day of the year. In 2012, that day happened to be January 9, my thirty-eighth birthday.

The purpose of that inauguration, my second, was to set a positive, hopeful tone. I wanted to have fun with the event to help us transition from the somber gloom of the previous four years. Mostly, I hoped to avoid an overly formal ceremony. What better way to set a new tone than holding the event outside, on city hall's front steps, in early January?

The imagery was pretty cool. I pictured a bitterly cold, blustery day: a wickedly fierce wind in my face, crystalized breath rising, and snow swirling and encrusting the microphone. I'd deliver a short, passionate speech about standing up to adversity and demonstrating the vigor and hardiness that define Duluthians. By confronting the elements, we would demonstrate our fearlessness in the face of whatever the world throws our way. We even found a guy willing to make a podium of ice to drive home the point.

But on January 9, temperatures hit a record high in the 40s, skies were blue, and the sun was bright. My plans were ruined. It was the most beautiful January 9 in our city's history. People ditched their winter coats and celebrated our good fortune. I was so disappointed. I was hoping for symbolic adversity. Now my only concern was whether a melting ice podium would make my speech soggy. 🛋

Laura as "Mayor of Pepperkakebyen"—the gingerbread village at Norway Hall

LAURA

One of the many things I love about Laura is how she cuts her own path. Like her parents and four siblings, Laura has a strong independent streak and a firm commitment to authenticity.

After we were elected, people started to refer to her as "Duluth's First Lady" and project their expectations onto her. But Laura, in her way, simply noted the phenomenon and continued to live her life precisely to her own expectations and no one else's.

I think Laura has handled public life beautifully: with grace, good humor, patience, support, and a willingness to carry extra burdens the job too often puts on a family.

While she has never sought the limelight, she has shone brightly whenever the attention has turned her way. People are drawn to Laura's relaxed and casual tone. Her quick smile and generous attention put people at ease. They are impressed by her calm sense of confidence.

She has blazed her own trail. She has defined the role in a way that best suits her personality and her private nature. I think people like that part of her most of all. I do, too.

"It's just a unique opportunity that very few cities have—to have something like this."

—Adam Sundberg

DULUTH TRAVERSE

Over beer at the Brewhouse, Adam Sundberg and Hansi Johnson began to describe their vision for a mountain bike trail system that would cross the entire city. They were advocating for their sport, and I recognized the potential for a project that would celebrate and highlight Duluth's unique strengths. Together we committed to building a hundred-mile, world-class, single-track system called the Duluth Traverse.

How many other cities …

» Are twenty-six miles long, allowing for a forty-two-mile linear trail connecting nearly all the major neighborhoods in the city giving broad access to the population?

» Are built on a hillside, providing ample topography for heart-pumping climbs and giggle-inducing descents?

» Feature spectacular views of the world's largest freshwater estuary and the world's greatest lake?

» Have eleven thousand acres of publicly owned green space spanning the city and providing a wide variety of ecological and aesthetic experiences?

» Have a well-oiled mountain bike club like COGGS, with three hundred passionate members that give back four thousand hours a year in volunteer time?

» Have young, local entrepreneurs, like the owners of Loll and Bent Paddle, who invest in a unique vision because they see outdoor recreation as healthy for their businesses, their employees, and their community?

When complete, the Duluth Traverse will be the only trail of its kind in the world. It will be an epic, backcountry single-track experience embedded into Duluth's unique urban environment, with access for riders of all abilities. It's also the foundation for what Duluth is becoming—a world-class mountain biking destination.

CITY COUNCIL

Great dramas play out in these chambers. City councilors wrestle with the difficult task of shaping the city's future, balancing competing interests. Historically, the council has been willing to make tough, necessary decisions that move our city forward.

I have tremendous respect for how councilors approach their responsibilities. The council has passed thousands of resolutions and hundreds of ordinances that have landed on my desk. While I've disagreed with a handful of their decisions, I've never used my veto. I believe that the relationship between the council and mayor is more important than any single item of disagreement.

NOT FIT FOR HUMAN CONSUMPTION

by Nathan N. LaCoursiere, March 18, 2015

For many years, Old Downtown was home to the well-known head shop Last Place on Earth, or LPOE. Owned by Jim Carlson, the business was located at 120 E. Superior Street—right in the heart of Duluth's Historic Downtown District.

During the summer of 2010, Carlson began selling addictive and harmful synthetic drug products commonly known and marketed as "legal alternatives," "incense," "bath salts," "watch cleaner," "pipe cleaner," and so on. The products were labeled "not fit for human consumption," though Carlson made no effort to hide his knowledge that customers were purchasing the products to get high. At the time, the nation was slowly waking to this new public health threat. Duluth had the misfortune of being on the front end of this emerging drug trend and swiftly became ground zero in the national war to stop it. By 2011, Carlson was selling to upward of 1,000 customers a day—to the tune of $16,000 in revenue a day or $6 million a year.

Nuisance conditions flowing from the sale of synthetics at LPOE quickly overwhelmed Old Downtown. Customers clogged the sidewalk in both directions every day, blocking access to neighboring businesses. Police calls skyrocketed. Duluth Police Department received 2,843 calls for service to the block over one 12-month period. Nearby building owners reported finding vomit, urine, and human feces in their entryways. Pedestrians were solicited, panhandled, and verbally abused.

The city responded quickly, calling on Carlson to end such a civically damaging trade. Carlson answered in the manner that would typify his defiance through three subsequent years of litigation, indictment, and eventual federal conviction and sentencing. He assumed the mantle of a freedom fighter, using the media to cast himself as a defender of individual liberties in the face of government overreach. Carlson further claimed that his drugs were legal (even when later chemical testing proved otherwise). Given the nature of synthetic drugs—which allow street chemists to quickly tweak compounds and claim they are not banned by existing drug laws—Carlson adopted an aggressive and well-financed legal defense. It was clear that in the absence of a creative, determined, multi-

early 2011, the city started building coalitions and strategies to tackle the problem on all fronts. Local law enforcement worked closely with public attorneys to gather evidence in support of public nuisance actions and criminal prosecutions. The city labored to craft ordinances broad enough to encompass synthetic drugs.

Events moved quickly. The city commenced its first public nuisance action in early 2012, obtaining an order requiring LPOE to pay city police costs for nuisance enforcement. In December 2012, Carlson was indicted by the United States Attorney's Office on more than 50 counts of violating federal controlled-substance and FDA laws. Carlson defiantly continued selling, resulting in two additional city nuisance actions and a city licensing ordinance that ultimately forced closure of the business on July 19, 2013.

The business never reopened. In October 2013, a federal jury convicted Carlson on 51 of 55 counts of violating federal drug laws. Carlson later was sentenced to 17½ years in prison. United States Marshals took possession of the business, removing the iconic signage from LPOE's façade and readying the building for sale.

The Historic Downtown District sprang back to life with the closure of the business, sparking anew the creative and artistic renaissance in Old Downtown. The city's creative legal and regulatory approach set national precedent. Cities from around the country have sought Duluth's counsel in tackling synthetic

CHARLIE BELL

Charlie Bell was a passionate community leader—a rare breed of person who dared to dream big then rolled up his sleeves to get the job done. He was fit and vibrant, full of energy and new ideas. His list of accomplishments on behalf of Duluth—especially for seniors, public schools, and business development in his beloved West Duluth—is long.

Charlie and I will be linked in local history because of the 2007 mayoral race, in which we agreed we would run for the same position but not "against" each other. That agreement allowed us to stay friends during and after the campaign—certainly unusual in the history of Duluth mayoral races. I'm still proud of that, and I know he was, too.

Leaders like Charlie Bell do not come around very often. His death in 2014 was a sad, tragic loss for his family, his friends, and this community. He leaves a lasting legacy and a model for community-minded business people to give back to the places they call home.

Handwriting Problems

They say that you can tell a lot about a person by examining their handwriting. For my sake, I hope "they" are wrong. Hopefully you've been able to read these first sentences, because I'm putting in a tremendous amount of effort to make it legeable just to prove to my co-workers that it is technically possible, it's just painfully slow and tedious. I mean, those first five and a half lines have taken me fourteen minutes. My fingers are cramping up in attempt to make letters that are generally independent of one another and of a size that "people can actually read," as it thinks an important consideration while writing. I'm honestly not sure why my handwriting is so awful. Thinking back I guess it's always been pretty bad. I blame it on poor technique since all five of my fingers are bunched together around the tip of the pen like five fat mobsters huddled around a tiny counter table. OK, OK – I'll rewrite that one... All five of my fingers are bunched together around the tip of the pen like five fat mobsters huddled around a tiny circular table. See? now you can go back to that previous sentence and you'll totally be able to read it.

Meeting fun and
interesting people is the
best part of the job.

COUNCILOR VS. MAYOR

When I leave office in January 2016, I will have served eight years as a city councilor and another eight years as mayor. I've always been fascinated by the power dynamics between the council and mayor in Duluth's strong-mayor system. Having served significant time in both offices, I've come to understand and appreciate how each role creates different perspectives within city politics and governance.

And I've started to wonder... if Councilor Donny Ness and Mayor Don Ness had been serving at the same time, what would they have thought about each other?

Here's what Mayor Don Ness might say:

> "Councilor Ness is a busybody. He creates unnecessary work and brings up symbolic issues, like the Patriot Act, that distract our focus from city responsibilities. He complicates simple issues, diving into them too deeply and drawing out debate, waiting to commit until he's heard every last perspective. I wish he'd just focus on his council votes. I like the kid, but he drives me crazy sometimes."

Here's what Councilor Donny Ness might say:

> "Mayor Ness is too disconnected from the council and our decision-making. Things move quickly, and we're not kept in the loop. As a councilor, I want to make a positive impact. I want to make a difference. But I don't feel the mayor is giving me enough opportunities, so I have to go out and make my own. I also gotta feel sorry for the guy. I mean, look how much he's aged in office."

Consider the six-month adventure of a single leaf.

FIVE-HUNDRED-YEAR FLOOD

The ground was already saturated from a cold, wet spring when yet another storm rolled into town. All evening and all night, a heavy, seemingly solid curtain of rain fell. You could hear the sustained density of the storm. It wasn't wild. There wasn't much wind or movement. It was relentless.

Ten inches of rain fell in just twenty-four hours. Streams swelled and overflowed their banks. Culverts and storm sewers that had survived a hundred years of weather were destroyed or blown out by a surge of water raging down our hillside.

By the next morning, chaos reigned, and we were in crisis. Homes flooded, hillsides slid away, and standing water obscured dangerous streets that would soon collapse. Every mayor imagines reacting heroically in a crisis. Now, with a crisis in front of me, I was hit with a surge of uncertainty and insecurity.

More than once that day, especially early on, as damage reports started coming in, I worried I wouldn't be up to the task. I had studied the Emergency Operations Plan, and I understood my responsibilities. But within that three-hundred-page action plan, there was not a single word about how the mayor was supposed to lead.

"What if I'm not up to the task? What if everyone clearly *sees* that I am not up to the task? What the hell should I be doing RIGHT NOW!?!?" A swirling torrent of issues pulled at and demanded my attention.

Then I realized that hundreds of Duluthians were responding to this crisis. Residents didn't need me to be a hero. They just needed me to do my job.

In the end, the hero was the entire community. Thousands of Duluthians fulfilled their roles with diligence and modesty. No one tried to be the star of the moment. No one tried to steal the limelight. This allowed the entire community to share ownership in responding to the crisis and starting the recovery.

Mother Nature hit us hard that summer but didn't dampen the goodness of our community. Instead, limitless compassion, courage, and selfless giving emerged. Neighbors went house to house, offering up their Shop-Vacs®, dehumidifiers, and time. People lent trucks to haul ruined, sodden materials from flooded basements and homes as families rallied together to do some post-flood version of barn raising.

The resilience of Duluthians then and now inspires me.

Laura and Don with Queen Sonja and King Harald of Norway

ROYAL VISIT

When Laura and I learned we would have the honor of welcoming the king and queen of Norway to Duluth, I couldn't help but think of great-grandfather Christ Ness, who immigrated to Duluth from Norway in 1905. I imagined him taking that long, uncomfortable boat ride to an uncertain future in an unfamiliar place. I wondered whether he could have imagined that a century later one of his descendants would welcome royalty from his old home to his new one.

I was fairly certain his heart would have swelled had he seen all the proud Duluthians—many whose bloodlines came from Norway and many whose didn't—who gathered at Enger Tower on a blustery day and warmed King Harald and Queen Sonja by flying, wearing, and waving thousands of Norwegian flags. While strolling and chatting with the king and queen that day, Laura and I were incredibly proud of our community and intensely conscious of our roles as the community's ambassadors. We felt buoyed by the outpouring of enthusiasm.

We learned later that most royal visits tend to be incredibly formal and tedious. I'm glad we could establish a fun, warm tone for their visit to Duluth. When we first met them, conversation was stilted and awkward, but by the end of the visit we were joking and laughing. A Norwegian Consulate representative told us that the Duluth visit was the highlight of their American tour.

Ice cave adventures
Cornucopia, WI (2014)

EQUILIBRIUM

Before the advent of social media, a small number of gatekeepers shaped perception of public figures. Successful politicians were able to create and cultivate superficial personas of success, popularity, and infallibility. "Staying on message," was the gold standard. Through confident repetition of narrow talking points and bold projection of leadership qualities, politicians could control and protect their images.

Social media has changed the landscape of public opinion in dramatic fashion. Politicians still using the old rules of engagement are exposed as disconnected or inauthentic. Ubiquitous social media has produced something like a free market for information that influences reputation. If a politician is presenting a traditional persona of infallibility that feels insincere or inaccurate to us, we call them out on social media. Conversely, if we feel a politician is not receiving the credit they deserve, we instinctively promote and support them. Eventually, this push and pull creates equilibrium in the market of public opinion.

Elected officials who haven't adapted to this new reality have suffered the consequences.

SOCIAL MEDIA

Social media is a modern mayor's most important tool. Deliver an instantaneous message to thousands of constituents with one click? Get feedback and make personal connections just as fast? I become weepy just thinking about the constituent-connecting power of Facebook and Twitter.

Those connections are vital. Every reciprocal share, like, and comment becomes part of how politicians and constituents get to know each other and exchange ideas. Most of my Facebook friends and Twitter followers are there because I show pictures of my kids, try jokes, take criticism, and generally interact like "a real, live human being." If I connect with people authentically, they'll be much more likely to engage with occasional policy and budget messages, snowplow and pothole updates, and economic development news.

BICYCLING THE HILLSIDE

The climb feels endless. Tattered concrete fills my field of vision—taunting and mocking my painfully slow bike ride up the hill. My legs ache and are starting to shake. My lungs burn and seem to collapse a bit more every time I turn the pedals over and try to suck in a great, heaving gulp of oxygen.

The front wheel wobbles for lack of momentum, forcing me to cross back. Now I'm shamefully zig-zagging across the steep avenue, which both relieves the burdensome pitch, but quadruples the length of the climb. There is a deep desire in me, immutable by logic or maturity, to ride the whole way, steep inclines notwithstanding.

Then the moment of kinetic equilibrium arrives in which the depleted energy of my legs can no longer overcome gravity's backward force and for the briefest moment my bike and I are stuck in suspended animation. I dismount at the very moment gravity begins to prevail. With humility washing over me, bike and I switch roles as I become the vehicle delivering the two of us up the hillside.

Pushing. More pushing. Still pushing. Finally I'm up the hill. Exhausted. Discouraged. Angry at whoever thought it would be cool to build a city like this. Life would be so much easier in a city built on a former cornfield. Then I turn around—it's really just a slight torso twist; a foot shuffle; a slow, exhausted, subtle pivot—and my perspective changes dramatically.

After forty years of hillside living, it is no less spectacular. Duluth stretches around the expansive hillside, nestled into dense forest and parks, overlooking the world's greatest lake.
No matter what my heart is doing before I turn to look, it swells with pride when I scan the horizon.

It's not just Duluth's hills that demand effort. The whole city challenges us to expend energy and develop endurance. We earn our loyalty to Duluth, and the effort creates an affection that folks who haven't lived here might not understand. The struggle of living on this hill shows us significance in everyday vistas.

SURPRISE SPEECH

> *(Here I am at yet another convention …what was this one about? Ok, here's the program …. The Association of Association Associates? What could that possibly mean?)*

Our next speaker was first elected in 2007…

> *(Wait—is that my bio? Am I speaking at this?)*

… please welcome Mayor Don Ness.

> *(Ok, ok, don't panic—just play it cool—but think of something to say!)*

Welcome to Duluth! You know here in Duluth there are some great …

> *(That's good, use all the general stuff—keep the energy high— what is this group called again? Association what?)*

And how about the weather today? It sure is (hot, cold, beautiful, miserable).

> *(Oh man, the iPhones are coming out—I'm losing them! Quick, start pandering!)*

What an amazing looking group—such energy in the room. I want to thank you for all you do back in your home communities as association associates, you make such an important difference to your community and your associations.

> *(Ok, they're warming up, but just barely, I'd better wrap this up before I lose them again.)*

Thanks for having your gathering here in Duluth, I hope you have a great time, and thanks for giving me the chance to say a few words.

> *(Oh man, that was awful.)*

A Tale Of Two Mayors

1. Former Minneapolis mayor R.T. Rybak is probably the most stage-divingest mayor there ever was.

Floats like angel!

Keeps smiling

100% rock star

hair remains amazing

The man could crowd surf a senior center Bingo night.

2. One time, conceding his defeat in the gubernatorial endorsing convention, he crowd surfed Carmody Irish Pub in Duluth.

Don't see this very often.

Losing with class.

His lithe frame made it surprisingly easy for patrons to toss him around the bar.

3. In 2012, both mayors Ness and Rybak were asked to introduce Trampled By Turtles at First Avenue.

Don. We have to stage-dive.

Uhh... Sure!

4. Ness' knowledge of stage-diving consisted entirely of **observing** mosh pits in the Duluth area, and **watching** 90's grunge-era rock videos.

Grew up in an era where a guy in flannel could land on your head at any time.

The 90's: Truly did smell like teen spirit.

5. After their introductions and to the fanatical cheering of the sold-out crowd, R.T. Rybak glided gracefully onto the crowd, smiling the whole way.

6. Ness, egged on by the band, caught in the spotlight, seeing no graceful way out, and against all better judgement, dove headfirst off the stage.

7. Unprepared for this level of impact, the first three rows were plowed over and knocked to the ground like tie dye bowling pins.

8. A lot of beer got spilled. Dusting himself off and leaving the crowd, he could only wonder:

SEEKING TRUTH

Politicians and pundits too often claim ownership of the truth.

Any claim of definitive truth kills curiosity and eliminates potential to learn. If we believe we're the ones with the truth, we no longer seek, we simply defend. We build fortresses. Rhetorical attack and defense become the only ways we know how to discuss issues. We're always fighting or preparing to fight.

National political figures have become notorious for projecting absolute certainty and confidence in their ideologies as truth and justice, then, in the same breath, condemning the opposition as absolute enemies of truth.

I don't own any truth. I try to hold lightly those ideas I think are true. Truth evolves. It changes with the world. It takes on so many layers of complexity and beauty and interconnectivity that no human mind can comprehend it, let alone own it.

So we seek. We are on a path of common discovery. As we share our perspectives on truth, we contribute to each other's understandings as we deepen our own.

Our lives can be dedicated to the discovery. What a beautiful concept: dedicating our lives to discovering truth we'll always get closer to and never fully attain.

Our living room. Each of the three kids blending into their surroundings—color, light, and shadow.

"*Politics is too serious a matter to be left to the politicians.*"

—Charles de Gaulle

CRAFT BEER CAPITAL

Let's take a moment to consider a poignant metaphor: American cities as beer styles.

It's an undisputed fact that most of the beer consumed today is weak, watered-down corporate beer—more accurately, weak, watered-down corporate beer *lite*. It's also true that a very large percentage of Americans live in communities that strive to create experiences as predictable, unimaginative, and bland as ubiquitous corporate beer.

I want to stress that despite having a taste for neither bland beer nor unimaginative communities, I don't believe there's anything wrong with other people liking them. Those beers and places to live are popular because a lot of folks want friendly, simple experiences. Who among us has not wanted some friendliness and simplicity in our lives?

But a small and growing segment of society is searching for life with uncommon—even challenging—flavor. Life that offers adventures and layers of complexity that might not be evident on the first sip. There's a thirst for authenticity, craft, and quality. Sometimes folks just want something different from the monoculture of corporate beer.

Duluth offers an IPA-style experience—bold and hoppy. It presents a bitterness that's off-putting to the uninitiated, but core to the experience for those who love it. There is a sweetness there— citrus maybe?—but it's a more complicated, interesting pleasantness. It's about quality over quantity; authenticity in a world of conformity; appreciation of our neighbors' craftsmanship. Not everybody seeks that, but for those who do, Duluth is a pretty great place to find it.

TAKE IT WITH YOU

One of my favorite mayoral duties has been a monthly guest appearance on the hilarious *Take It With You* live radio theatre podcast. I've appeared in every episode except one, when I was traveling in North Carolina. We wanted to keep the streak alive, so we had planned to audio tape my part. Then inspiration struck—Laura could play my part! The concept was that mayors have a special trick that allows them to be in two places at once—so I was both in Asheville *and* at the show (played by Laura).

Laura nailed the performance (of course)!

TAKE IT WITH YOU
live radio theatre from Duluth, MN

THE SCRIPT

BILL: So, wait Mr. Mayor, you're ALSO in Asheville right now? What are you doing *there*?

LAURA (as Don): Oh you know, sitting in my hotel room, flipping through family photos, drinking a glass of milk, hugging a pillow, and thinking about how much I love my wife, Laura.

BILL: Now, don't take this the wrong way, Don … but your wife is smokin' hot.

LAURA (as Don): Umm … well …

MARY: C'mon Bill. You know this is a touchy subject for the mayor … I mean, it can be a real burden to be married to a woman who is SO much more attractive, intelligent, personable, and kind. I mean, Don, I've heard you say it many times before, that you married WAY above your station in life … Am I right, Mr. Mayor?

LAURA (as Don): Well, yeah, but … I mean, I hold my own. *[Pause for a few seconds of uncomfortable silence.]* Just kidding! I'm in WAY over my head!

OTHERS: *[A series of quick jabs under laughter]* Laura makes Don look like a … a … a … Arial Lift Bridge troll … Yeah, it's like he won the hot lady lottery, ya know? … Don is so far out of his league, he's, like, playing in the wrong sport ….

BILL: *[In the din of laughter and in the rhythm of throwing out these one liners]* I'd like to kiss Laura Ness right on the mouth. *[dead silence]* What?

BLAKE: Not cool, Bill. That's the mayor's wife you're talking about.

ST. LOUIS RIVER

Excerpts from the 2014 State of the City address:

There's no question that if not for Lake Superior, Duluth would be defined as a river city—but it doesn't have to be one or the other. In my mind, Duluth should be defined by both the world's greatest lake *and* the world's greatest freshwater estuary.

Residents along the St. Louis River corridor value their distinctive living experience. Many corridor communities feel like small, close-knit villages rather than urban neighborhoods, fostering a strong sense of belonging and pride among residents. Each neighborhood features distinctive strengths, but the

common thread is access to an amazing natural resource that is too often overlooked in Duluth: the St. Louis River.

The opportunity for growth in the St. Louis River corridor represents a larger movement that's gaining momentum. People are drawn to Duluth, and cities like Duluth, by extraordinary natural beauty, connection to the outdoors with the perks of a big city, and a unique work-life balance that Duluthians take for granted but millions of hard-working Americans yearn for.

BEST OUTDOOR TOWN

Duluth won *Outside* magazine's 2014 Best Towns contest, a month-long online tournament to determine which one of sixty-four outdoor-friendly cities is America's best place to live. More important than the victory is the extraordinary sea change that made the win possible. People are proud of Duluth, and that hasn't always been true.

People from all over the country proclaimed their love of Duluth during the competition. I joined community members to proudly highlight our world-class outdoor recreation and natural beauty that compare favorably to much larger and more well-known cities.

The victory is a tangible manifestation of Duluth pride and enthusiasm that have been growing for a decade. It's important because people invest in homes, business, personal skill sets, and careers when they live in cities they feel confident and optimistic about.

For decades, cynical voices defined our city. Too often, we simply accepted Duluth's inability to fulfill its potential. Today, optimistism defines Duluth's voice, pointing us in a confident direction.

Is this change real? Ask yourself this question: Do you think Duluth could have won this contest twenty years ago? Not a chance.

Babies dropping from Heaven! Fortunately, I was in the
backyard to catch this one. He's turned out to be a keeper.

WINNERS

To fully appreciate this essay, go listen to the song "Winners" off the Trampled by Turtles album *Wild Animals* (2014).

I first heard Dave Simonett of Trampled by Turtles play "Winners" at an intimate Red Star solo show on a cold winter night. Dave's songwriting always presents imagery that is deceptively subtle and saturated with complex feeling. The song's line, "Pretty little city built on a hillside" is an obvious nod to Duluth, but "Winners" is no promotional jingle—it's much more complicated and interesting. It's a song about character forged through youth that was intense and dichotomous. It's equal parts about fighting for breath and breath being taken.

The yearning is plaintive and innocent—the appeal of someone practicing, studying, building something that does not yet exist and trying to make sense of it all while simultaneously, desperately trying to hold on to each brutal, imperfect moment. Even in its softest turns of phrase, the song portends loss: losing the beauty of first experiences—of what was alive and authentic.

Somehow, Dave uses the city to embody this emotional dissonance. He describes fire in the sky and ice on the beach. Amazing music in a tired, crumbling space. Pretty little city, but there's nothing coming in.

People have deep emotional connections to Duluth that are impossible in most cities its size. That emotion is often equal parts love and frustration. Authentic love is not one-dimensional. It has to challenge us; we've got to work at it.

We make ourselves vulnerable when we open our hearts to the expanse and terminality of any given moment. Then, too often, life cuts deep with pain or disappointment. We learn to hedge our bets, seek safety in conformity, and limit what makes us vulnerable. I suppose it's maturity. Maybe it's self-preservation.

To me, "Winners" is a sad, nostalgic song. It conjures complex and conflicting feelings about watching a moment slip quickly away and loving this city so hard it sometimes hurts. It captures a time that was equal parts grit and beauty, struggle and joy.

PAY INCREASE

Awake until 3:00 a.m., I pondered scenarios. After a career spent exclusively in public service, Laura and I had very little saved. Now relief from our financial worries was being offered. All I had to do was take it.

I asked myself big, uncomfortable questions. I thought about the kids, about my family and political future, about public perception and the decision's impact on my ability to lead.

Should I accept a $20,000 (twenty-five percent) raise? Or should I decline it?

I thought about my many tough, unpopular decisions that required other people to make financial sacrifices for the common good. I thought about Duluthians who struggle to get by. I questioned whether taking the raise would undermine perceptions of my credibility. I unsuccessfully wrestled with dozens of scenarios, hoping to figure out how I could accept more money and feel okay about it.

Then a simple solution became clear. I would decline the raise.

Later that morning, Laura confirmed what I felt: our life would be better if we declined the increase. We agreed that regardless of short-term drawbacks, declining the raise was best for our family. Our faith grounded the decision, and we believed we were planting seeds that will bear fruit for the kids as they grow.

I felt relieved—tremendously relieved—that we would simply live our life. Exactly as before.

Presidents age two years for every year they're in office. Mayors age a year and a half for every year they serve. According to that math, I have gained four to six extra years, which has helped me make up for the decade or so I was behind.

NESS 2016

BECAUSE
people who run for
PRESIDENT
SELL MORE
BOOKS

Don
Ness

BUY MY BOOK NOW!
Paid for by the Ness 2016 Exploitatory Committee

NESS *for* PRESS-

ident of the United States of America

DULUTH, MN—As part of my book marketing strategy, I'm announcing the formation of an "exploitatory" committee to exploit an unsuccessful run for President of the United States of America.

I'm joining in solidarity with my political brethren and sistren who are also running even though most of us have ABSOLUTELY NO CHANCE of EVER becoming president.

"But Don," you may ask, "why would someone run for president if they intend to lose?" Good question. Because I want to sell a bunch of these books, and my marketing team tells me even an insincere presidential bid could help me unload at least 32 more than I otherwise would.

The only problem is, even intentionally running unsuccessfully for president can be really expensive. So I'm seeking a billionaire (but ideally two) who can funnel at least $10,000,000.00 of their "free speech" into my campaign coffers or toward a few Ness for President independent super PACs I will totally know nothing about (wink wink).

Essentially, I hope to extract maximum benefit from the campaign process while avoiding the risk and heavy burden of actually becoming president (which, let's be honest, seems like an awful gig). In doing so, I hope to join a long list of Minnesotans who have run for the office and failed. In my case, failure is an important part of my success. Is this a joke? Of course it is. But so is the whole process. Don't act like I'm the first "candidate" to treat a presidential campaign as a joke.

Look. I'm not kidding. Under no circumstances should you actually vote for me.

Failing at this selfish plan to be unsuccessful could result in me becoming president. That would be seriously uncool.

BECAUSE … *you know* … THE FUTURE (*& book sales*).

TEN YEARS WITH LAURA

I tend to think about the past in ten-year chapters.

A decade feels so elegant. A year is too short to fully contextualize events and growth. Beyond a decade, memories look fuzzy and events become irrelevant to the present day. Ten years is just right: rich in changes and opportunities for clear recollection.

After our first decade together, Laura and I reflected on changes we had experienced. As individuals and partners, we had aged and evolved. We became parts of one, then two, and finally three little people. Like every couple we know, we've navigated rough times. We grew apart and back together, stronger for the struggle. Public life raised some of the hurdles, but most of our ups and downs have been common to any two people always learning how to share a life.

I love Laura more today than I did on our wedding day, and on that day I was head over heels and couldn't comprehend loving her more. We know each other more completely than we did then. We've accommodated each other's weaknesses, and we've learned the subtle strengths of each other's character.

In these next ten years, our whole family will gradually move away from public life. Laura and I will deal with a household defined by teenagers. We'll experience heartbreak and uncertainty, but I feel optimistic and excited because I'll be walking the path with her.

THE MILLENNIAL GENERATION

Never before have a generation's values and priorities more closely aligned with what Duluth is and can be.

GRADUATE

Finishing my master's degree from The College of St. Scholastica took me ten years. All sorts of distractions (and excuses) kept me from completing it sooner: fatherhood, mayorhood, husbandhood, watching football-on-Sunday-afternoonshood.

I found tremendous value in the classes and coursework, so I pushed forward and eventually got it done. When I finally prepared to graduate, St. Scholastica President Larry Goodwin asked me to speak at commencement.

Every year, thousands of commencement speakers seek to capture the significance of transitioning from scholarly life to the real world. Their lofty, poetic vocabulary and themes comprise messages of hope, beauty, inspiration … and clichés. After one or two speeches they all—every sing-songy, stilted, schmaltzy collection of challenges and platitudes—sound identical. In different ways, the same is true of almost every political speech. I decided to have fun with the stereotype by delivering a melodramatic compilation of the most common clichés.

Your dreams represent the best and brightest dreams of your future … dreams. As one door closes, we go forth into a journey only our dreams could imagine a key that would unlock a dream of a peaceful future … tomorrow.

Tomorrow, which is the first day of the rest of your future lives … (wait, no, tomorrow is the second day of the rest of our lives.) The actual first day of the rest of your lives is today (which then continues tomorrow), but today we can dream about tomorrow.

We dream of a journey of living your life to the fullest potential, which is just the beginning … of future dreams … to believe in … and to dream about.

In summary, I will quote the great Whitney Houston, in verse … (ahem) …

"I believe the children are our future / teach them well and let them lead the way.
Show them all the beauty they possess inside / give them a sense of pride to make it easier.
Let the children's laughter remind us how we used to be."

Inconceivable!

Despite the many hundreds of hours I spent with Jim Oberstar, this will be my most indelible memory of him.
After dinner, he went upstairs to read to Ella and James (who was named in his honor). It was a wonderful moment.

CELEBRATION OF JIM'S LEGACY

On May 3, 2014, our country lost a great leader. A strong voice. A man who dedicated a lifetime to the never-ending task of striving for a more perfect union. Jim Oberstar loved his country and loved serving the people of Minnesota in Congress. We owe him a tremendous debt of gratitude.

Working for Jim sparked in me acute awareness of his powerful force in shaping our nation's future. I believe Jim's impact on northeastern Minnesota is more significant than any leader's in our region's history, and we are right to celebrate that proud legacy of accomplishment.

Jim was a friend, mentor, teacher, and steady, loving hand when we needed him to be. Above all, he was a good man. His staff is still loyal to him because he was a caring boss. They still love him because he was their friend. That's a special combination.

One of my favorite quotes is by Dr. Thomas Fuller: "Great and good are seldom the same man." It's such a challenge for people to achieve both. How fortunate we are to know a man who truly embodied both.

Thank you, Jim. Thank you for being *great* and, more importantly, for being *good*.

DECISION NOT TO RUN

In November 2014, I was enjoying public life more than I ever had. The city's economy was humming: unemployment at a fifteen-year low, huge construction projects underway, and an increasingly strong reputation in the region. In city hall we had assembled an amazing team, the organization was coming off a string of important accomplishments, and our budget resulted in a property tax decrease. I enjoyed going to work every day, and I was proud of our accomplishments. It was hard for me to imagine how it could get any better.

So I announced I wouldn't seek reelection.

I know, I know. It doesn't seem to make any sense. Yet for me it was so clearly the right decision. I've enjoyed this experience so much. I love the work, the challenges, the people. Looking back, even the struggles have felt satisfying and constructive. Not because I enjoy struggling, but because I love the city we have struggled for.

In the moment I felt content—the moment things felt under control, the moment I realized my energy was directed a little too much toward celebrating and justifying the status quo—I realized it was time for me to step aside. Contentment is the enemy of progress. A new mayor, with fresh perspective and a different set of strengths, will help the community maintain forward progress we've all started. 🚌

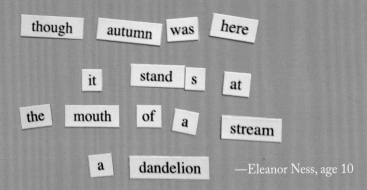

though autumn was here
it stand s at
the mouth of a stream
a dandelion

—Eleanor Ness, age 10

MY LAST HOMEGROWN AS MAYOR

Confidence is such a powerful force. Duluth has discovered a newfound pride and can-do attitude that is fueling our recent renaissance. Without a doubt, Duluth's best days are yet to come.

CONCLUSION

So there you have it. It's a pretty modest story, really, and in a way that's the point. You don't need to consider yourself extraordinary to make a difference in community-based politics.

During my career, I've moved quietly and subtly in directions that contradict expectations and conventional political wisdom. Sometimes that meant not attacking others. Sometimes it meant not promoting myself. Other times, it meant just having the patience to let situational emotions subside. And almost always it meant understanding that part of my job was to accept criticism (fair or not) of my actions and judgment (accurate or not) of my intentions. When tempted to act like a jerk or say mean things, most often I haven't.

To summarize: I'm pretty good at not doing stuff.

When I entered politics in my twenties, I was excited to see what would happen if I rejected convention and just consistently, sincerely worked hard to improve Duluth. I knew that approach might not work, but I figured folks would maybe recognize and support my earnest efforts. It worked pretty well.

When everyone else is making a hard sell, the soft sell stands out. In a field dominated by aggressive fighters, a policy wonk is appreciated. When a whole bunch of politicians bombard folks with anger, cynicism, and fear, a voice of sincere optimism can provide a welcome reprieve.

I've found modest success in political life by choosing to be sincere, then holding to that choice with discipline and patience. Even though sincerity is simple, it's not always easy, and I was grateful that once my approach became apparent, talented and energetic people emerged to help. Genuine effort within local government inspired reciprocal genuine effort within the community. Sincerity attracted sincerity.

The strength of my campaigns? Volunteers. The basis for our success in city government? City staff. The health and wellbeing of our family? Laura. The city entering a virtuous cycle? Contributions from 86,000 other people. I just sort of suggest ideas then try not to get in the way. Some stick and some don't, and I'm always surprised how often that works.

Generosity from others has been the central theme of my public life. It's come in multiple forms: willingness to take a risk on an unproven kid running for city council then mayor; support for a mayor making unpopular decisions; enthusiasm for contributing to Duluth's renaissance.

Our recent success in Duluth has been based in optimism. We've demonstrated the power of confidently owning and solving problems. But I can't shake a debilitating pessimism toward federal governance.

The whole federal system is broken, and powerful interests profit from its brokenness. The dysfunction is newly built into the very structure of our democracy, from the laws that govern our nation to the tragic interpretation of our Constitution that gives the rights of human beings to non-human legal constructs, namely corporations.

That system of power and cynicism has created a disgustingly lucrative industry that encourages and promotes combative ideologues into leadership and has discouraged thoughtful community-builders—the kinds of leaders we need—from entering or staying in public life. We're fortunate that most Minnesota leaders in D.C. are thoughtful and engaged. Unfortunately, they're part of an ever-shrinking minority.

But I have hope.

I'm especially hopeful about the generation of leaders coming of age today. I believe they will define political and governmental norms that foster long-term national good instead of perpetuating a game that benefits only narrow interests. If these new leaders commit to change then stay sincere and patient in their efforts, they'll build a critical mass that shifts our country's course for the better. A movement to make these changes could succeed quickly. People throughout the country are hungry for it. They're desperate for a better brand of leadership.

When that movement takes hold, I want to be part of it. Not as an elected official, but as someone whose stories, experiences, and support can help young leaders see possibilities, find inspiration, and maintain motivation. I believe we can all foster a new generation of leaders who govern with confidence, optimism, and sincerity.

THANK YOU KICKSTARTER SUPPORTERS!

Self-publishing a full-color book is an expensive and risky proposition since we need to print in volume in order to drive the cost down to a somewhat reasonable point. There is no practical print-by-demand option for full-color publications. Filling the book with professional photography, original art, and 150+ editing-intensive essays would normally be prohibitively expensive. A project like this depends on a great deal of generosity, and our Kickstarter campaign has allowed us to pay a lot of talented people a little bit of money.

All Kickstarter funds have been used to pay talented local people for their work. Ideally, book sales and not our home equity (seriously) will recoup design, production, printing, distribution, and various other costs.

To everyone who contributed: thank you. The book you're holding exists only because of your generous support. I appreciate it more than I can say.

Special thanks to (from top left): Pascha & Abbot Apter, Adele Hartwick, Nathan Bentley, Gregory Benson, Sean Dean, Lynn Marie & Jim Nephew, Kelley O'Leary, Terri Kragseth, and Matt Musel (not pictured).

Thank you.

Many thanks to (from top left): Arend Sandbulte, Ben Damman, Brian Daugherty, Bruce Stender, Craig Chilcote, Dave Hoops, David B Wheeler, Edwin K. Hall, Emily & Gary Kalligher, Geno Sung, Howard Klatzky, Jennifer Turner, Jill & John Doberstein, Jill Rowlison, Erin & Jon Otis, Kathy Ponder, Kyle Krueger, Lindsay Anders, Mark Emmel, Mike & Dawn Erlandson, Scott Gilbertson, Sherry Hall, and Nancy & Tom Saxhaug.

Thank you.

And thank you to Kristen Ahlm, Josh & Amy Allen, Jeff Anderson, Karen Rapp Anderson, Mary Kay Bailey, Sarah Bamford Seidelmann, Jesse Bandelin, Shane Bauer, Matt Billings, Heidi Blix, Derek Bolme, Sherry & Mark Boyce, Natalie Brown, Jeff Bullert, Scott Burns, Nick Campanario, Nancy DeArmond, Melissa Williams Delamartre, Carmel & Christopher DeMaioribus, Gabriel Douglas, Peter Eckman, Nancy Eilefson, Sarah Eilefson, Jennie Emeott, James Eubanks, Lee Francisco, Rebecca Fredrickson, Greg & Bev Gamradt, Kandi Garrison, Beth Gauper, Rees George, Mat Gilderman, Wallace Goulet, Amber Haglund-Pagel, Elissa Hansen, Joanna Helder, Sarah Herrick, Kate Horvath, Patrick Huot, Cpl. Tyler Patrick Johnson, Grant Johnson, Troy Johnson, Bill Kimbler, Dan Kitzberger, Sandi Knutie, Anna Korpi, Eldon Krosch Jr., Melissa La Tour, Andy Langager, Kristin Larsen, Kris Larson, Nick Larson, Jacob Levine, Ted & Juliane Link-Oberstar, Amanda Lisiecki, Anita Lurye Silver, Jack Lyons, Scott Lyons, Danielle Magnuson, Jennifer Marksteiner, Marie-Laure McKee, Serina Modec-Halverson, Jared Muskovitz, Richard Narum, Elizabeth Norné, Doran Nurm, Sara Nutter, Monica Oberstar Weber, Jim Ojala, Matthew & Ericka Olin, Lynnette Olson, Tim & Emily Opacich, Jeremy Osgood, Kala Pedersen, Ross Perko, Cathy Podeszwa, R, Tara Radosevich, Walt Raschick, Rissa Roberts, Rita Rosenberger, Amy Sader-Brown, Sam, Drew Sandquist, Erik Sather, Heidi Schallberg, Lelia Scheu, Jen Schnabel, Lisa Schrader, Tyler Scouton, Samuel Seering, Andrew Sharpe, Tim & Judy Sheriff, Angela Shields, Sarah Shilman, Singing Waters, Duke Skorich, Linnea Stephan, Jana Studelska, Surges Family, Carl Svendsen, Andrew Thompson, Terese Tomanek, Wendy Underwood, Matias Valero, Forrest Vodden, Joe & Erin Warner, James Wheeler, and Mark Winson.

page 3
© H. Brian Rauvola

page 4
© Andy Miller

page 7
© Hattie Peterson

page 8
© Kip Praslowicz

page 9
© Barry Yanowitz

page 11
© Derek Montgomery

page 15 © Tim Clay
timcclay@live.com

page 16
Grandma Marge
© John Schadl

page 17
© Andy Miller

page 18
© Duluth News Tribune,
Clint Austin

page 20
© Jake Gunderson
Paean Photography

page 23
Pam Kramer
© Michael K. Anderson

page 23
Helen Horal

page 23
Howard Klatsky

page 23
Sandy Sandbulte

page 23
Yvonne Prettner Solon
© Michael K. Anderson

page 23
Bob Hartl

page 23 *Bob Powless*
© Michael K. Anderson

page 23
Cal Benson

page 23 *Jim Oberstar*
& Bill Richard

page 23
John Heino

page 23
Bruce Stender

page 23
Kamal Gindy
© Jeff Peabody

page 23
David Wheeler

page 23 *Kathy Heltzer*
& Eddie Crawford

page 24
© Duluth News Tribune,
Bob King

page 25
© Aaron Molina

page 27
© Don Trueman,
Paramount Pixels

page 28
© Duluth News Tribune,
Sam Cook

page 29
© Duluth News Tribune,
Derek Montgomery

page 30 © Bridge
Syndicate, Becca Moen

page 31
© H. Brian Rauvola

page 32 (all faces)
© H. Brian Rauvola

page 34 © Tim Clay
timcclay@live.com

page 34
© Duluth News Tribune

page 35
© Jess Belwood

page 35
© Jess Belwood

page 35
© Jess Belwood

page 35
© Jess Belwood

page 37
© John Schadl

page 38 *"A rare and fragile bird"*
© Adam Swanson

page 40-41
© Joe Klander

page 44
© Anne Victoria

page 47
© Brian Barber

page 48
© Derek Montgomery

page 51
© Deb Carrol

page 52 *Sienna Effinger*
© Scott Lunt

page 52 *Tim Nelson*
© Rich Narum

page 52 *Scott Lunt & Sarah Heimer*

page 52
Devin McKinnon

page 52 *Mark Lindquist*
© Scott Lunt

page 52 *Christa Lawler*
© Rich Narum

page 52 *Jason Beckman & Molly McManus*

page 52 *The Alrights*
© Rich Narum

page 53
© Scott Lunt

page 54
© Shawn Thompson

page 56
© H. Brian Rauvola

page 59
© Dennis O'Hara

page 60
© Brian Barber

page 61 *David Ross*
© Derek Montgomery

page 62
© Duluth-Superior Area Community Foundation

page 64
© Beau Walsh

page 65 *Chris Homan & Carolyn Reisberg*
© Zach Kerola

page 66
© Dennis O'Hara

page 69
© Duluth News Tribune, Clint Austin

page 71 Courtesy of Luke Nadeau

page 72
© Dennis O'Hara

page 75 Courtesy of Wellstone Action

page 76
© Don Davis

page 80
© Michael Birawer 2012

page 83
© Kenneth R. Kollodge

page 86 © Larry Dunlap Summerfields Photography

page 86 Courtesy of perfectduluthday

page 86 Courtesy of perfectduluthday

page 86
© Brandon Wagner

page 89
© Taylor Bjork

page 91
© Michael K. Anderson

page 93
© Andy Miller

page 96
© Joe Klander

page 99
© Jeremiah Brown

page 100 *Tony Bennett*
© Andy Miller

page 100
© Kip Praslowicz

page 101 *Al Sparhawk & Steve Garrington*
© Rich Narum

page 101 *Jamie Ness*
© Rich Narum

page 101 *Scott Lunt*
© Rich Narum

page 101 *Hattie Peterson* © Nate Minor

page 101 *Adam Depre*
© Rich Narum

page 101 *Fred Tyson*
© Rich Narum

page 101 *The Keep Aways* © Rich Narum

page 102
© Dennis O'Hara

page 106
© Duluth News Tribune,
Steve Kuchera

page 109
© Joe Klander

page 107
Nancy Norr

page 107 *Mark Emmel*
© Duluth News Tribune,
Amanda Hansmeyer

page 107 *Dan Russell*
© Duluth News Tribune,
Amanda Hansmeyer

page 107 *Steve Greenfield*
© Duluth News Tribune,
Amanda Hansmeyer

page 107
Pat & Carrie Heffernan

page 107
Carl Crawford

page 107 *Jeff Corey*
© Michael K. Anderson

page 107 *Linnea Stephan & Pat Mullen*

page 107 *Rick Ball*
© Michael K. Anderson

page 107
Kristi Stokes

page 107
Xavier Bell

page 107
Nathan Bentley

page 107
Dave Montgomery

page 107 *Duke Skorich & Patty McNulty*

page 110
© Bridget Riversmith

page 114
© Wisch Photography

page 114 Courtesy of
R.T. Rybak

page 115 *Zachary Stofer* © Mike Scholtz

page 115 *Gabriel Douglas* © Rich Narum

page 115 *Chad Lyons & Ryan Nelson*
© Andy Miller

page 115 *Brittany Sanford & Bob Monahan*

page 115
Terry McCarthy

page 115 *Todd Gremmels* © Rich Narum

page 115
Adeline Wright
© Alison Aune-Hinkel

page 137 (all photos)
© Aaron Molina

page 143
Portia Johnson

page 115 *Hung Nguyen*
© Andy Miller

page 138
© Michael K. Anderson

page 143
Jason Wussow

page 115 *Chad Lyons*
© Rich Narum

page 139 *Charlie Parr*
© Andy Miller

page 143
Heidi Bakk-Hansen

page 115
Marc Gartman

page 141
© Amanda Teague

page 144
© Derek Montgomery

page 116
© Jess Belwood

page 143
Will & Sally Munger

page 146
© Brian Barber

page 118
© Dennis O'Hara

page 143 *Mona Chelsek*
© Michael K. Anderson

page 148
© Dennis O'Hara

page 128
© Brandon Wagner

page 143 *Debbie Isabell
Nelson & Bill Majewski*
© Michael K. Anderson

page 151
© Steve Forslund

page 129
© Michael K. Anderson

page 143 *Steve O'Neil
& Mary Murphy*
© Michael K. Anderson

page 153
© John Heino

page 130
© Dennis O'Hara

page 143 *Gene McKeever*
© Rich Narum

page 154
© Jess Belwood

page 133
© Duluth News Tribune,
Bob King

page 143 *Sonny Halbecka*
© Michael K. Anderson

page 155
© Paul Walsh

page 135
© Derek Montgomery

page 143 *Alex Guiliani*
© Michael K. Anderson

page 156
© Steve Forslund

page 136 Courtesy of
St. Scholastic Monestery

page 143 *Karin Swor*
© Michael K. Anderson

page 157
© Kip Praslowicz

page 136 Courtesy of
O'Neil Family

page 143 *James Gittemeier*
© Michael K. Anderson

page 158
© Deb Carroll

page 160
© Rene Rhodman

page 162
© Zach Kerola

page 164 (both photos)
© Duluth News Tribune,
Clint Austin

page 165
Karen Sunderman

page 166
© Andy Miller

page 168
© John Schadl

page 169
© Hansi Johnson

page 172 *Tim Kaiser*
© Rich Narum

page 172 *Sarah Krueger*
© Rich Narum

page 172 *Nikki Moeller*
© Rich Narum

page 172 *Matt Mobley*
© Rich Narum

page 173 *Walt Dizzo*
© Andy Miller

page 173 *Jerree Small*
© Rich Narum

page 173 *Crew Jones*
© Rich Narum

page 173 *Marc
Gartman* © Zach Kerola

page 173 *Social Disaster*
© Rich Narum

page 173 *Big Wave
Dave & The Ripples*
© Andy Miller

page 174
© Jeremiah Brown

page 177
© Michael K. Anderson

page 179
© Joe Klander

page 180
© Cirrus

page 182
© Jeremiah Brown

page 184
© Duluth News Tribune,
Bob King

page 185
© Preflash Gordon

page 185 *Laura Gapske*
© Preflash Gordon

page 185 *"Smackmeister"*
© Preflash Gordon

page 185 *Kelly Mullan*
© Preflash Gordon

page 186
© Brandon Wagner

page 188
© Brian Rauvola

 page 190
© Andy Miller

 page 192
© Craig Samborski

 page 192
© Rich Narum

 page 193
© Rich Narum

 page 193
© Rich Narum

 page 194
© Brian Barber

 page 196 Courtesy
of John Biasi

 page 197
© Duluth News Tribune,
Bob King

 page 197
Dan Hartman

 page 197
Todd Fedora

 page 197
Emily Larson

 page 197
Al Franken

 page 197
Lynn Fena

 page 197 Rick Nolan
& Jeff Anderson

 page 197 Jen Schultz
& Sharla Gardner

 page 197
Patrick Boyle

 page 197
Jennifer Julsrud

 page 197
Howie Hanson

 page 197 Tony Cuneo
© Michael K. Anderson

 page 197 Roger Reinert
& Layla Reinhart

 page 197
Nancy & Mark Rubin

 page 199
© Joe Klander

 page 202
© H. Brian Rauvola

 page 204 Courtesy
of Duluth Chamber

 page 205 Courtesy
of Duluth Chamber

 page 207
© Sarah Krueger

 page 209 © Naomi
Yaeger-Bischoff

 page 210
© Hansi Johnson

 page 212
© Hansi Johnson

 page 212
© Hansi Johnson

 page 212 Adam Sundberg
© Hansi Johnson

 page 212
© Hansi Johnson

 page 212 Hansi Johnson
© Clint Austin

 page 214
© Andy Miller

 page 219
© Derek Montgomery

 page 220 Charlie Bell
© Michael K. Anderson

 page 221 Stephan
Witherspoon © Ivy Vainio

 page 223 Tyler Scouton
© Zach Kerola

page 227
© Chris Monroe

page 237
© Arna Rennan

page 239
© Steve Forslund

page 228
© Duluth News Tribune,
Bob King

page 238
Jane & Ken Gilbert

page 240
© Chris Monroe

page 228
© Kip Praslowicz

page 238 Brian &
Kaylee Matuszak

page 243
© Hansi Johnson

page 228
© Kip Praslowicz

page 238
Kathleen Busche
© Trudy Vrieze

page 246 Brian 'Lefty'
Johnson © Andy Miller

page 228
© Duluth News Tribune,
Bob King

page 238 Bill Gronseth,
Jen Julsrud, Randy Bolen,
Daniel Fanning

page 247
Courtesy of Bent Paddle

page 228
© Kip Praslowicz

page 238
Maajiigwaneyaash

page 247 "86211"
© Adam Swanson

page 230
© Paul Walsh

page 238
Jana Studelska

page 247 Eddie Gleeson
© Andy Miller

page 230
© John Heino

page 238 Heather
& Scott Millis
© Rich Narum

page 248
© Crystal Pelkey

page 230
© Dennis O'Hara

page 238 Rod Raymond
© Brett Groehler

page 250
© Brandon Wagner

page 233
© Rich Narum

page 238
Dave Hoops

page 252
© John Hatcher

page 233
© Dennis O'Hara

page 238
Dan Neff

page 254
© Zach Kerola

page 234
© Andy Miller

page 238
Greg Benson

page 257
© Duluth News Tribune,
Bob King

page 236
© Chris Monroe

page 238
Eric Swanson

page 258
© Jon Dyess

page 259
© Aaron Molina

page 259
© Aaron Molina

page 259 © Adam
Bettcher Photography

page 259
© Andy Miller

page 262 © Adam
Bettcher Photography

page 264
© Andy Miller

page 266 Courtesy
of The College of
St. Scholastica

page 267
© Brian Rauvola

page 268
© Hansi Johnson

page 272
© Dennis O'Hara

page 274 *Dave Carroll,
Dave Simonett*
© Andy Miller

page 274 *The Farsights*
© Walt Dizzo

page 274
Red Mountain
© Maxwell McGruder

page 275
© Dan Dresser

page 275 *"ChickeNess"*
© Adam Swanson

page 275 *Boomchucks*
© Kip Praslowicz

page 276
© Kim Randolph

OTHER CREDITS

Cover
© Hansi Johnson

page iii
© Sophia Peterson

page 290
Bob Monahan

page 290
© Chris Monroe